LOVE YOUR GIFTS

LOVE YOUR GIFTS

Permission to Revolutionize Authenticity
in the Workplace

Angie McCourt

To request permission, contact the publisher at angie@angiemccourt.com.

Paperback ISBN: 978-1-7376831-0-0
eBook - Kindle ISBN: 978-1-7376831-1-7
Audiobook ISBN: 978-1-7376831-2-4
Library of Congress Control Number: 2021920433

First paperback edition October 2021

Edited by Runaway Publishing
Cover art by Lauren Diamond
Photography by Shawna Benson Photography

Published by Authentic Me Revolution

www.angiemccourt.com

DEDICATION

To my beautiful son Brandon who showed up every day as his authentic self. You had the biggest heart and always welcomed others in, no judgment. You created a full life in your 25 years here on earth. I'm so proud of you for the person you were, your passion for everything you touched and for the healing you created for others. I love you and miss you every day. Stay wild my moon child.

Sometimes you've got to let everything go – purge yourself. If you are unhappy with anything... whatever is bringing you down, get rid of it. Because you'll find that when you are free, your true creativity, your true self comes out.
—Tina Turner

CONTENTS

FORWARD

Authenticity. A character trait that is highly admirable that so many strive for yet struggle to achieve in their daily lives. People at their core want to be genuine and people long for those around them to be real, so what could possibly be holding them back? Well, a multitude of reasons that are convoluted and dynamic and that take time to unpack and understand, such as everyday environment, various life experiences, lack of confidence, long held beliefs in what should be often engrained starting in early childhood, or let's be real, fear of judgement from others and often ourselves. These are things every person struggles with at some point in their lives regardless of what may appear on the exterior. Add in the complexities of living in a 24/7 world of cultural spin cycle and the need to consistently outdo the latest trend and it only gets harder. Now add in the additional elements of the workplace and the pressures that come with increased global reach and never-ending focus on the bottom line. To many, it can be hard to keep up, let alone see the light, and even harder to stand out with the authenticity we so deeply strive for. But worry not, there is a way out and each of us have gifts readily available inside that just need to be nurtured to thrive. Some gifts are obvious at the onset such as the ability to influence others or write a great proposal, but many, and often more important gifts, such as empathy, intuition and applied patience are less appreciated even though they are the most powerful. Take the traditional ingredients of a dessert favorite, a fluffy key lime pie...eggs, limes, condensed milk, a buttery, graham cracker crust, which combine together in various measurements to form a really good pie that anyone would be glad to serve. But the more we measure and combine with a methodical approach and add ingredients not so readily obvious, such as a little lemon, we start to truly get the best of what could be accomplished. Lemon in a key lime pie, you say? Yes, not necessarily appreciated or understood at first but try it...it will blow you away. So, good thing for you bakers, shakers, and business makers, this book is exactly what you need to understand your hesitation, hone in on and harness your gifts, and activate and apply them with precision. The end result...you find your way to professional utopia.

The author of this book, who happens to be my dear friend and colleague of many years, Angie McCourt, is gifted with the ability to help people realize their best selves and find their true purpose, with an approach that is supportive, uplifting, empowering and exciting. She is smart, kind, humble, compassionate, trustworthy and makes development practical and fun! She truly is one of a kind and those who know her are better because of it and this world is a better place because Angie is who she is and does what she does to uplift others. The book is a testament to her many, many gifts and her desire to help you find and harness yours. I am proud of you my friend and wish all of the readers all an amazing journey!

Kristi Kirby

INTRODUCTION

Let's talk about your gifts! The ones that are not typically included in your performance reviews or career development conversations. Those not recognized for the gifts they truly are. Those not realized for the impact they have on others, business, community, and life as a whole, and even those viewed as negative. OK, let's go there.

Patriarchy has developed a "system" of approach for thousands of years, but it's starting to crumble. The reason is that we are realizing the gifts we have (our birthright) are valuable and should be recognized in today's world (including the business world). If I hear one more time that decisions should be solely based on numbers, I'm going to puke. Yes, puke! It makes me sick to my stomach when my own intuitive gifts are not recognized or trusted. Hello, I used them in business pretty successfully for twenty-seven years. And yes, I've stated this without fear; I trust my gut! Of course, I use numbers too, but honestly, there is NEVER a case where the most effective decisions can be based solely on numbers. Why? Because situations change at the speed of light, many future outcomes cannot be predicted numerically, and people are still important in how they deliver or execute their experience, credibility, critical thinking, and big-picture capacity.

I'd like to bring to light those "other" elevated gifts. The ones that truly make a difference with our teams, business, leadership, and effectiveness in the hope (yes, I use this word almost daily now) others will start to embrace their gifts, talk about them, not hide them, or feel ashamed when an authority figure gives their opinion (based on that ole patriarchal system). I want to bring light to your gifts and how special they are.

I'm very passionate about this topic because I lived it for a long time. I also broke free from it and allowed my elevated gifts to shine regardless of whether others were ready to receive them, and even if I wasn't recognized for the impact I made. It was the right thing to do, and it is who I am. My experience in corporate environments is only a part of the story. The past five or so years I've gone on a personal deep-dive journey prompted by curiosity and sparked and motivated by the connections I made with mentors, teachers, courses, books, and articles across many modalities. It's a whole other world! It has given me tools, healing, and insight into what needs to change. Too many of us fear showing up to the workplace with our authentic self and have been placed in "the box." I would love the honor of freeing you from that box so you, too, can show up as your authentic self and overcome fear and limitations to live a happier life in and out of work.

Here is how I define the most-used terms in this book. Let's start with our mind. There are three basic areas of our mind, the conscious, subconscious, and unconscious.

I love Ariana Ayu's explanation of the three.

The conscious mind is the part we're aware of and think with. It is easily manipulated (i.e., you can change your mind when presented with a compelling argument), and it's the part of our mind we are most familiar with. When someone refers to "my mind" in a conversation, this is usually the part they're speaking about.

Our conscious mind makes up about 10 percent of the overall. We do analysis, think, and plan, and use our short-term memory with our conscious mind.

She continues:

The unconscious mind is the creator of dreams. Its job is to sort and organize the millions of pieces of data you've been exposed to. I always think of the unconscious mind as a file clerk in a gigantic room full of file cabinets. Some rare bits of information get dismissed as trash, but most of it gets filed away in case it's useful later.

I saved the subconscious mind for last because it is the most complicated, and for our purposes, the most important. The subconscious mind is where mental programs are created and carried out. If you want to change the mental programs you're running, the subconscious mind is where you 'll need to focus. [1]

Our subconscious mind is the other 90 percent and includes our long-term memory, emotions and feelings, creativity, developmental stages, spiritual connection, and intuition. We form habits, relationship patterns, and addictions in our subconscious mind. It also performs our involuntary body functions.

Our egoic mind is not the enemy, although sometimes I get pissed off at mine. It's "an ambitious sense of self that drives us to accomplish things," according to Pearl Zhu. When it's healthy. It's the voice in our head and the one that isn't all that useful, but pretends to be. I tend to want to shove it in the "box" for allowing me to stay there for so long.

Pearl goes on:

Ego is tied to self-esteem and balance. Too much ego has one thinking too much of oneself—minimizing, marginalizing, and dismissing the perspectives of others. Too little ego has one not believing in oneself. The pendulum can swing to either side. [2]

The ego mind is always in battle with our intuition. Intuition is defined by the *Oxford English Dictionary* as the ability to understand something immediately, without the need for conscious reasoning and

[1] Arian Ayu, "3 Parts of Your Mind That Affect Your Ability to Make Decisions," *Inc.*, April 22, 2016, https://www.inc.com/ariana-ayu/3-parts-of-your-mind-that-affect-your-ability-to-make-decisions.html

[2] Pearl Zhu, "An 'Ego' Mind: Good or Bad," *Future of CIO, 2015*, accessed 2021, http://futureofcio.blogspot.com/2015/01/the-ego-mind-good-or-bad.html

a thing that one knows or considers likely from instinctive feeling rather than conscious reasoning.

Anastasia Belyh states:

Your intuition helps you identify your purpose in life. Since your intuition is attuned to your subconscious, it can point you in the right direction and help you identify dreams that are aligned with your core values and your true sense of purpose. People who rely on their intuition are more open to new ideas. [3]

Next are the influences we have been exposed to over time. Conditioning and old programming are the influences that entered our subconscious throughout our life from family, teachers, society, media, church, and government. These influences can be generational, intentional or unintentional, just information, experiences, or what we take in through our senses. Nothing is filtered, yet they create our beliefs and impact how we think and what we do today. Here's the kicker: they may not even be true. Yup. Our subconscious mind does not determine if thoughts are accurate or true. It just stores them and shares them back with us when we poll for information. Where did the system come from? Thousands of years of programming, conditioning, control, and staying between the lines. I call it the patriarchal system, but it has nothing to do with gender. It's what was created not only by government, but by church, school systems, and any other system formed to create consistency.

Throughout this book I'll reference the "box," especially in the workplace. Here is my definition of the "box." The "box" is a conformed structure and set of "rules" we are expected to live in, create from, and believe in. It can end up becoming our identity. It is a way to keep us in line, predictable, productive, and just like everyone else. It's what we go to when we fear not being accepted or like everyone else.

---

[3] Anastasia Belyh, "How Intuition Helps Us Make Better Decisions,"- *Cleverism*, September 25, 2019, https://www.cleverism.com/how-intuition-helps-us-make-better-decisions

Life is an initiation. That is my way to describe our journey, beginning as one of lessons, learning, expansion, and suffering. It's how we can navigate life in a way of exploration and growth instead of shrinking in fear.

Have you ever felt like there was more to you? Your authentic self or true self is who you truly are as a person, regardless of your occupation and the influence of others. It is an honest representation of you. Your inner self is the hidden ally you have with you always and who you can tap into for clarity, guidance, and answers. It's what guides you to be an even better version of yourself every day. It's what guides you through the lessons you are here to learn.

Finally, I'd like to define elevated gifts. This is my own terminology I use to describe the next level of gifts I see in people and have experienced myself that are nontraditional to the workplace. They are not recognized for the value they bring or for the impact they have. These are more complex gifts, yet ready for you to connect to. Or maybe you already have, but they are not appreciated by others.

How to use this book: in most sections there is a "make the shift" exercise that helps to do the inner work and integrate change. Pick those that you resonate with the most. I've created a workbook that includes all of the "make your shift" exercises you can use to track your work. Head to angiemccourt.com/loveyourgifts/ to download the workbook. You can also use a journal to capture your thoughts and feelings and as a reference guide. Add in your observations as you go through your journey.

Part 1 Your Subconscious is Your Superpower is all about identifying the things that can hold us back from being our authentic self in the workplace, sharing how we rewrite our stories, addressing limiting beliefs, recognizing limitations and how to overcome them, digging into letting go of what has been conditioned and programmed in us, and opening ourselves to possibilities. We will address the "box" as well as limitations. It's important to identify what distracts us and how we spend our energy.

We will review identity and how it can impact us. An important piece to consider is mindset and our preferences. We will also dive into judgment and expectations.

This first part gives clarity to all of the things we have the opportunity to change, leading to freedom and liberation when it comes to work and life at times, opening ourselves to new ways of being and living. It also clears space to allow for our elevated gifts to be activated and shine. Dig into the exercises even if you might think or feel you don't need to. You may discover something underlying that could open up everything for you.

In part 2 you will meet your authentic elevated gifts. I call them elevated because they are not traditionally on the checkbox list of companies who recognize the skills, talents, and capabilities of their employees. These are typically the gifts that just make someone stand out. Sometimes they are not recognized, and many times they end up becoming expected instead of appreciated.

Why do I call them gifts? I view gifts as innate—we're born with them—they're within us and are something we can expand and tap into. Plus, they are special. Capabilities and skills just don't do them justice. I love that we can spend our entire lifetime discovering our gifts and talents. This gives us a never-ending journey to keep our eyes wide open to what is now blossoming in us and also what will blossom in the future, continuing on and on.

These gifts are in us all, and they come out when we feel safe, authentic, and accepted for ourselves. When we are not worried about rejection by others, these gifts shine. When we are not competing and comparing ourselves with those around us, these gifts shine. When we validate ourselves instead of seeking external validation, these gifts shine. Not only do they shine, but using our gifts allows us to lead teams in a refreshing way, innovate in leaps instead of steps, and bring big impact to how and what we do for customers, employees, community, and humanity.

Breaking old programming happens within each of us and is one of the ways these gifts can shine, as well as being supported to take that journey by company leaders and culture. How can we recognize those gifts and what do they look like? That is what I'll cover in this part. My interpretation and design of each of these gifts are based on my observations of others, my own journey, and conversations with others about how important these gifts are—and especially now. I've given each gift an archetype (name) and defined the attributes for ease of relating to these elevated gifts. You will more than likely start to see even more gifts show up in and around you once you are open to new beliefs and appreciation for these gifts. You can even come up with your own labels/titles for these gifts. It's fun!

I'm not into labeling, but I almost feel it's necessary to get the point across about these gifts, mostly to bring awareness for those with them and those who may have taken them for granted in team members. If you look at culture and why one team may work in a completely different way with different results, peel back the onion a bit. I bet you'll find there are special gifts floating within the dynamics of the individuals and leading the teams with more pizazz.

Part 3 Activating Your Gifts is all about how to take the work you have been doing to overcome limitations so you can unlock your elevated gifts. This is where we build. We set the foundation that will help you live in your own authenticity, unveil and activate your elevated gifts, and understand how to tap into the tools that you can use to navigate yourself and the workplace.

Are you ready? I'm so excited to be your guide on this journey, and I look forward to your expansion and to seeing you shine. We will first explore who you are and go deep into the areas that can influence your authenticity and elevated gifts. Then it's all about personal power and what it takes to find and keep it. The methodology we will use to bring your elevated gifts forward and the tools that will help you do so will be something you can carry forward every day. As your gifts take shape, we will dive into activating and adapting them along with how to work with the "challenges." We close with the opportunity to revolutionize the appreciation of your elevated gifts and authenticity in the workplace, and a call to action to start the conversation for change.

I'm grateful to guide you on this journey, and my hope is for you to tap into your gifts through your authenticity, elevate what you already have, and share your findings and results with others. It's time to revolutionize the workplace!

PART ONE
YOUR SUBCONSCIOUS IS
YOUR SUPERPOWER

1

WHY AM I IN THE BOX?

Conformity is the jailer of freedom and the enemy of growth.

——John F. Kennedy

Fitting Into the Box

In this chapter I'll address fitting in or being fit into and how that translates to the "box" in the workplace. It's that dreaded presumptuous thing we have all been put into starting with school and definitely in the corporate environment. I really feel there are two ways we can be: authentic or not. There are many pieces of ourselves that may make us feel comfortable in our authentic skin, but in certain situations, not so much. One of the biggest struggles I myself have gone through and so often see others go through is that of holding onto our authentic self in the workplace. The box has a major impact on our ability to do so, and we tend to not even realize it.

How we begin the process of seeking a job can unfold in many ways, including being our authentic self or not. I've hired people over the years who showed up in both ways. It's not that hiring someone who is not their authentic self during the hiring process is a bad thing for the hiring manager. Sometimes it ends up making their job easier—remember that box they need to put them into. But the issue comes later with the person not being able to be their authentic self and trying to keep the mask on all of the time. It's miserable.

Regardless of whether employees are hired with a new company as a fresh start or are beginning a new career out of school, corporations tend to try to put everyone in a box in order to control them, simplify expectations, and create predictability. The issue is that it's a killer of authenticity, genuine talents, productivity, creativity, and even happiness. There is some subconscious survival mode that kicks in when we want to be successful, earn income, or make a good impression that pushes us to want to fit in. So we jump in the box. Fitting in has been something most people strive for all of their lives—to be accepted, validated, valued, and ultimately loved. It's a human thing. It tends to create challenges down the road once a person realizes they are in the box and want to get out. Of course, this is not something corporations want to see. It ends up causing others around you to see the light as well. You might even be labeled a rebel—ha!

The need to fit in is why we jump into the box without really understanding long-term consequences. We formulate our "work" personality and try to do everything we think is expected. I'll get deeper into expectations in another chapter. For now, let's just focus on fitting in and wearing a mask that we really did not consciously sign up to wear. I literally remember stating to people that I had my work personality and my home personality for many years during my thirties. I guess once I hit forty, I really didn't care as much about the masks. However, why wait to ditch the mask? I'm calling this out as a potential challenge on the journey to authenticity in the workplace because it is. If you have to wear a mask to feel like you fit in, it uses a ton of energy and is exhausting. When I refer to "fitting in" in the workplace, it ends up really becoming about what you say, to whom, how you behave, and what you allow to shine through. Think about when you only bring into conversations those things you feel match others, are accepted, and help you to fit in.

In reality, most of our fitting-in masks are based on assumptions we create through observation and others' perspectives. Do they really help us fit in? I bet bringing in the word trust at this time brings on a powerful reaction. The reason trust is so important on the journey to authenticity in the workplace and ditching the mask is because it is foundational. The fact that we must work with our coworkers and leaders tends to create this pressure to show up in a way that is accepted, regardless of the trust built in those relationships. I've found when I don't have a trusting relationship with someone in the workplace, it creates withholding, extra energy spent on protecting myself (or them), and wearing a mask that is not the authentic me (or them). When I do have trusting relationships, I don't have a desire to fit in, it's just me that shows up to conversations and the work.

One way to jump out of the box and bring in your authenticity is to build trust. Many years ago I had a new director, and I was really struggling with him asking so many questions and what I felt was challenging me on my ideas and plans. I took on so much stress from this situation and finally went to someone else to ask for advice. This person gave me the best advice I have ever had on the topic of trust. He said, "Ask yourself what this person's intentions are; if they are good, then you can trust them." Whoa, this immediately changed how I was feeling in my physical body. Of course this person's intentions were all good, they just had their own process in seeking to understand. I already knew the information and process and they didn't. I needed to give them space and time to consume and understand it in their own way. I have given this same advice to others who struggled with trust in their work relationships. Trust becomes a window of opportunity to ditch the desire to fit in and, hence, the mask. It provides the opportunity to get one leg out of the box as well. It is really important on the journey to authenticity due to the importance of not only you trusting others, but them trusting you.

Make the Shift

Determine what mask you are wearing and a way to begin exiting the box.

1. Write down how you show up to work on a daily basis. This could be organized, decisive or not, frazzled or put together, all-knowing, productive, full of ideas, closed off or open to others, personal or strictly with the professional skin on (or what we tend to presume is the professional skin), and prepared (even though you may not be).

2. Write down how you are in the home setting using the same type of categories as work.

3. Find the differences between the two settings, and what stands out most to you. How can you shift to just being your authentic self rather than putting so much pressure on yourself to be something you're not?

In this exercise we are trying to determine the difference between your work and home personalities. It's so much easier to just be your authentic self versus creating masks based on what you think is a way to fit in or be accepted and respected. On the reverse side of us creating masks to fit in, corporations have a checkbox that influences this behavior. Let's dive into this next.

Checkbox Limitations

Let's dive into the checkbox in the workplace. The checkbox includes areas like how you dress or style your hair (physical), how you interact with others and react to change (personality), positive response and interactions (attitude), the words and approach you use to share ideas (communication), respecting the chain of command (hierarchy), how you ask questions and collaborate in meetings (engagement), the way you do your work (process), your performance statistics against goals created by management with rarely any real backing or input (results), your ability to create value (within the defined box), and how you share your success (humility).

What is interesting is the shift many companies have made to work values, yet the checkbox still exists and conflicts in many cases. They now look for a strong work ethic, dependability, responsibility, positive attitude, adaptability, honesty, integrity, self-motivation, motivation to grow and learn, strong self-confidence, and some are also seeking entrepreneurship. These are fantastic, but how each person shows up in each of these work values should not have specific expectations carried over from the old traditional checkbox. What this means is that companies can't define the result they expect from the employee, or it will probably not be the absolute best result. Authenticity plays a big role here in that each person is indeed different in how they approach situations, communicate, and share ideas. The more we compare them to the checkboxes, the less they will be able to show up with their most effective self.

If you've ever received a performance review, you can grasp the checkbox concept. The expectations of how you fit into these key categories of skills, behaviors, and results can be pretty cookie-cutter. It's time we expand this checkbox and how we appreciate the ways each employee can show up. Not only are we setting obscure expectations for those who may be doing a good job, but we are also holding back and misguiding those who are outstanding performers.

The traditional practice of managing people is just that—managing. The more authentic way of utilizing this key role in companies is as a coach. Coaches are very different in practice because they engage uniquely with each employee. Instead of providing yet another solution using the checkbox of career path, skills-building, feedback prompts, and increasing visibility, they tune in to where the employee is on their journey. They guide them more intuitively and put accountability on the employee to take the actions to help themselves. This is a big area where authenticity is suppressed, both with the "manager" and employee. In an authentic relationship between manager and employee, there would be open dialogue about struggles and ideas to make improvements (team and self). Feedback loops run both ways and the hierarchy is dissolved in order to build trust and impact.

The checkbox can also hold employees back from a fulfilling career path, as I've seen so many times. Feeling the need to fit into the checkbox also keeps employees on a specific path laid out by many others before them. It's the ladder approach versus a trellis approach to career path. I had the journey I never expected, and it was amazing! It was not linear, nor was it planned out. It was about expanding skills and experience through challenging roles and crossing functional areas or departments. I've appreciated the opportunity to have positions across many different departments, as this expanded my knowledge of the company, expanded my network, and increased new skills and experience. I love coaching folks on how to look at their skills as transferable. When you take a look at your skill strengths and where you have gained experience and match up those you will need in a new role, you'll see many transfer over. Yes, there may be some new areas or skills you currently don't feel as confident about, but that's the exciting part—the challenge.

The professional development checkbox is another outdated approach to personal and professional growth, keeping folks in the box that ends up actually limiting their potential. What I mean by the professional development checkbox is that there are specific categories that everyone should follow, expand, and make improvements on including collaboration, strategy, self-awareness, communication skills, delegation, empowerment, motivation, time and energy management, decision skills, working with uncertainty, etc. These are all fantastic to recognize as areas of opportunity to focus on improving. However, the challenge is that the majority of these areas should not have a one-size-fits-all expectation of end state on the growth journey. Typically, success is defined by the leader's expectations or mirroring of what they feel they portray. Everyone is different, and when folks feel like their authenticity is being suppressed in order to mirror and match the leaders' traits and behaviors, they become frustrated and may feel like they have hit the ceiling. When their nontraditional gifts are not recognized and appreciated for what they bring to teams and the business or role, it causes disconnect, resentment, fear, and a negative outcome to the original intention of professional growth. In part 3 I'll offer a new way of approaching the professional development checkbox and growth that is not so judgmental and limiting.

Make Your Shift

Write down your skill and experience strengths and compare them to what you think is needed for:

1. Your dream job
2. The job you "are next in line for"
3. Something (job, business, industry) you don't feel confident in pursuing.

(Note: if you're early or new in your career, think back a decade—you've been in training your whole life, so don't exclude your high school and college experiences.)

In this exercise did you see the correlation and the few jobs that pose gaps? Now you have a quick game plan started for what you should focus on building. Ask for special projects and own a dynamic career path. This exercise should also have shown you that you ARE ready for the next position and you DON'T have to be perfect at the job before you start it. Break away from the checkbox and feel your authentic self and desires.

2

LIMITATIONS BEFORE YOU EVEN GET STARTED

Tell your story with your whole heart.
———Brené Brown

Telling Your Story: Résumé

Résumés are interesting and it's such a challenge for applicants to crack this nut. There is a box that is very limiting around résumés and the tradition of sharing only your experience and education. Honestly, I stopped looking at education on a résumé over the last five or more years of hiring. Instead, I looked for WHO this person is and how they can bring passion and ownership to the business and team, and the potential they have for growth and expanding skills as well as leadership (not just a title or direct reports they had). It's amazing how many early-in-career employees have spent hundreds of hours volunteering or creating new communities or passion companies/projects, and those never show up on a résumé. Why not? It's who they are and what they believe in. It's about their story and evolution of growth and determining their values.

As part of the Exploratory Lab Boot Camp I cofounded with Pat Gehant seven years ago, we work with college students to break through the guidance they receive from campus resources. Here is what they are typically told to keep them in the box: create a one-page résumé, showcase education first, don't include unpaid internships, anything from high school, or any talents/crafts/sports, and NO volunteer work. Basically, what this does is limit the story the applicant can tell, and they look just like every other person who has submitted a résumé for that job. There has been a shift that hiring managers have made over the past five or more years where education isn't as important as potential and soft skills (including critical thinking).

Here are a few examples of creating stories with the students versus their one-page sterile résumé.

This is a conversation with someone I'll call Rob.

Me: What interests do you have?

Rob: I was a competitive boxer for the past nine years.

Me: That means you were up early, did daily workouts, and had disciplined nutrition, right?

Rob: Yes, I would work out before and after school.

Me: Great, that says a lot to me about how committed you would be to a job. What else?

Rob: I started a coding club for middle-schoolers last year, and it's been a great success.

Me: You specifically started it? Why did you do that?

Rob: I saw a need since there aren't many in the Tampa Bay area.

Me: That shows leadership, no fear of taking on new endeavors, you are resourceful to get it going, and committed to keep it going.

Next is Jarod.

Me: Why did you start down the technology path?

Jarod: I did an internship where I installed Cisco routers for a company and liked it.

Me: I don't see that on your résumé.

Jarod: It wasn't a paid internship, so I was told not to include it.

Me: That is a critical piece to your story. Why did you do the internship to begin with?

Jarod: I was part of a robotics team in high school and I learned a lot and our team went to a worldwide competition, where we placed third.

Me: I don't see that on your résumé.

Jarod: I was told not to include it because it was in high school.

Me: That tells me about your curiosity, commitment, and no fear to try something very new and is a great accomplishment. It needs to be included as part of your story.

Next is Rachel.

Me: Wow, you have many clubs you belong to. What roles do you play in each?

Rachel: I am president of this one, fundraiser lead on this one, etc.

Me: Why not elaborate on the roles you play and what you've helped those organizations accomplish?

Rachel: I was told to keep my résumé to one page and didn't have room.

Me: What type of career do you see yourself going into?

Rachel: Sales. I want to sell in technology.

Me: That's interesting because nothing on your résumé tells me you are competitive or an influencer. What else have you done before college?

Rachel: I was a competitive tennis player growing up.

Me: Now that shows me your competitive side. Why is that not on here?

Rachel: I was told not to include anything from high school.

Me: Well it's a big part of your story, defining who you are today and the training for life you have gone through. It needs to be included.

Applicants telling their story is so important because it gives perspective to the hiring manager about who they are and not just what they've learned or done. The résumé guidance from company human resources (HR) teams can be limiting as well, and not aligned with how hiring managers make their decisions. There is so much opportunity here to focus on creating better alignment and a space for future employees to show up as their authentic self from the beginning of the process.

The guidance from executive recruiters is all over the place as well. For executives who haven't actually had to interview for a job for years to now create a résumé with all of their roles, special assignments, and achievements can be quite long. Some recruiters want to keep it short and summarized, and some want to see detail. The most challenging part is for the applicant to share their story including how they lead and drive vision, strategy and execution. Résumés don't really provide a good platform to do so. We need a change!

Make the Shift

Review how you are telling your story?

1. Pull out your résumé and review it. (Hint: if it's been a while, update your format.)
2. Look for where you are showcasing WHO you are.
3. Find what's missing from telling your story.
4. Determine what impacts you have made, and how you can showcase your skills.
5. Ask someone to look it over and give you feedback.

Telling Your Story: Interview

Another limitation is in interviewing. There are many methods managers are taught to use in interviewing, but it becomes a structured exercise and not authentic or intuitive. Authenticity limitations around interviewing can end up being such a disconnect in hiring the best candidate. Many hiring managers are seeking authentic applicants, but the information they receive and seek is based on the old system. Inauthenticity of the hiring manager, lack of experience in interviewing, personal bias, being taught one method of questioning technique, using scripts, and not reviewing actual success with that hire after they are established can create a cycle of bad hiring. When hiring managers don't hire often or don't have much hiring decision experience, it can create not only a limiting experience for them and the candidate, but can also lead to a bad decision.

Sticking to the résumé as a guide to diving into examples of past experience can only limit exploration of the person. I had a particular interview in the past of an internal candidate where everything on the résumé had nothing to do with the type of experience needed for the position she was applying for. I simply asked, "What makes you want to go into a sales role when most of your background is operations?" She replied that she enjoys engaging with customers. I dug deeper. In which roles did you engage with customers?

"When I was a bartender and server for six years," she replied.

I said, "Oh, I don't see that on your résumé."

She replied, "Well, I didn't think it was relevant."

Guess what? I used that path to explore her ability to prioritize, solve customer issues, check her sense of urgency, and success building relationships. This would not have even come up if I was following a script or only basing questions off the résumé. The bigger question is, why do folks feel they can't fully show up with all of their experiences on their résumé?

Another example of the limitation to show up fully through this process is community and volunteer work. I was interviewing another internal candidate whom I did not know well, but she was applying for a position that would have been a promotion. As we dug deeper, she shared one key bit of information that opened up the door for exploration. It was an off-the-cuff comment, but so important. We went down the path of her role in a very significant nonprofit organization in the area and the leadership role she played. I was floored. Why did she not share this in her résumé or as an example in interview questions? I knew that the organization was heavily involved in the community and that leadership roles were like full-time jobs. New insight about her capacity, organizational skills, leadership, and commitment made her stand out from the other candidates. Without that it was a closer race.

I enjoy a more conversational interview style with emphasis on exploration versus telling me about this job or that job or this project or that project. It makes a difference to bring a sense of comfort to the interview so the candidate can be their authentic self. Self-evaluation questions give insight into confidence, collaboration ability, ownership, and more authentic evaluation of the role they played in a particular outcome. If the interviewer can expand out to a bigger picture to explore a candidate more genuinely, the amount of relevant information could actually prove successful. It's important to be able to ask questions that dive into experiences and transferable skills and be able to understand how they transfer to the job at hand. This is where critical thinking on behalf of the interviewer can be a limitation to get the best outcome. If we interview in a box, we will hire in a box.

There is such an opportunity to improve and change from the old structured ways of interviewing to allow for both the interviewer and candidate to be authentic and engaging in exploration versus a structured or scripted and limiting conversation about the candidate and/or job. Most candidates know what typical questions will be asked in an interview, so in reality, they have something prepared for each. I like when candidates can bring in honest challenges, outcomes that are both good and bad, and engagements with others good and bad and explain how they handled each of these. A perfect interview with all fluff and positives is as irrelevant as a bad job description or a clone résumé.

Make the Shift

Hiring managers and recruiters can make the shift by:

- Receiving training of different types of interview styles.
- Conducting group interviews (two managers as a mentored approach) until the newer interviewer feels comfortable.
- Preparing better for interviews including being able to articulate the company's vision/mission/values and the job's outcome expectations and not just the tasks/role.
- Sending interview surveys or evaluations to ensure the entire process of interview setup, conduction, and follow-up are successful (regardless of whether the candidate was offered the job).

Make the Shift

Candidates can make the shift by:

- Going back to the résumé section about building your story and thinking through many different types of situations where you have made an impact both inside and outside of work.
- Avoiding wearing a mask to the interview because you feel you have to in order to get the job. You'll regret it down the road. If the interviewer or company is not the right fit for you, it's better to find out now. Why would you want to work for a company or manager that isn't a good fit?
- Taking your time answering questions. Pauses are important. Quiet space is important. Don't fill it!

- Being authentic. If you don't know an answer or have a good example, ask if they can come back to that one. Also, share how you handle the bad along with the good. This is real.

This chapter on limitations was really to take a stab at some of the dysfunctional challenges with old systems and processes that really don't allow candidates to show up authentically and puts both hiring managers and candidates in the box. Be authentic, be yourself and find the match (both ways) that best fits you, your values, and commitment.

3

WHAT'S YOUR ROLE?

Things move along so rapidly nowadays that people saying: 'It can't be done,' are always being interrupted by somebody doing it.
——Puck Magazine

Limiting Job Descriptions

The limitations of bringing your authentic self into the workplace come in many areas, but it could start with the very first step of determining a job you wish to pursue. There are definitely old ways of carrying out the process of creating job descriptions that actually don't align with how companies are doing the work, setting expectations, and measuring results.

Let's get into job descriptions and how they are utilized inside and outside a company. Most job descriptions detail what is required in daily duties and expectations for performing a job. They typically include the most optimal employee doing the job and create a box employees can expect to sit in. Job descriptions are important to have in order to attract the right candidates, weed out those not qualified, and clearly set expectations.

There are many flaws with using the old system of creating job descriptions that impact not only the candidate pool, but also how candidates show up and apply. It starts with showcasing specific and unique expectations for positions that many candidates exclude themselves from applying for because they don't have every single skill or experience that is so-called required. This limits the pool of candidates. Most hiring managers don't actually make their decisions based on that list of requirements because they know the actual day-to-day responsibilities could change. This is a big issue with job descriptions, because they are not up-to-date with ever-changing roles and outcomes employees are expected to perform or skills they are expected to expand on. Another disconnect is that the hiring manager has changed their criteria for hiring decisions to be more based on fit, potential, initiative, and soft skills. Those typically are not emphasized in the job description.

Those candidates willing to take a chance that the job they think they will be doing is something they will indeed be doing then apply. Many times they adjust their story and résumé to accommodate the job description to get past the "gates" of software and HR screenings. Having to play the system is frustrating for candidates and, in reality, do we truly know how many fantastic candidates actually make it through this process or are stopped at a gate? Better alignment between hiring managers and recruiters is really important, along with regular reviews of job descriptions and ensuring the right one is used for a particular job. There are so many different outcome-based roles crammed into the same titles to reduce maintenance and try to create simplicity that it impacts the flexibility of the evolution of jobs and needed skills. This also risks candidates not truly being qualified for the actual job.

Another limitation around job descriptions is the fact most of them do not include consideration or direction of cross-industry experience or transferable skills. This also is a big gap in interviewing skills (hiring manager), which we'll discuss in a bit. When companies do not take the time to do this, they end up with the same candidate pool over and over (basically recycling employees within their industry). In reality, there are many folks early in their career and at different stages of career that want to make a change. If you only look at job descriptions and industry experience, the really great candidate is missed. There are so many skilled folks in the financial industry (including investments), insurance industry, and creative industries that transfer over to technology industry roles, for example. Not every role inside of a tech company is a technical role (actually most are not). I always loved hiring what I called fresh blood from not only outside of the company, but outside of the industry by taking a bigger view of the candidate's transferable skills, industry challenges they had, and their potential.

Job descriptions that are dreamy-sounding jobs can in reality be boring, boxed-in jobs that the employee ends up finding miserable. Overstating a job is just as bad as understating it. I like to see companies set job descriptions with a bit of a growth window or a progression which provides a view to the candidate up front to let them know that they have growth potential within the same role. This increases the candidate pool and provides deeper discussion during interviews around the potential the candidate brings, plus their desire for growth and development. It also gives the new employee an opportunity to start their job right away without so many boundaries (sitting in the box). Another approach is to use more vague pools of descriptions, and as candidates are reviewed via résumé or interview, the reviewers and interviewers determine where the candidate will best fit versus depending on the candidate to figure out if they are a good fit for a specific role. This is an option where expansion in business and teams is significant or when standing up a new team.

Unless job descriptions and this part of the process changes, there will continue to be gaps in how candidates and new employees can show up authentically.

Make the Shift

Hiring managers with HR teams can make the shift by:

1. Discussing what is most important for employees to bring to the table—truly what is most important for them to be

successful and deliver the outcomes needed. This should not be a cookie-cutter approach, as typically roles change often.

2. Identifying what can be considered on-the-job training and is not necessarily needed to qualify for a job.

3. Deciding what the hiring manager finds most important to their decision in hiring, whether soft skills, finding or solving problems, critical thinking, initiative, or ownership.

4. Rewriting job descriptions with less structure and more clarity of needs and grouping the most important versus those that are nice to have that would indicate a standout candidate.

5. Determining if more or less job descriptions and titles are needed based on the outcomes employees are actually expected to produce.

6. Setting up a process to review job descriptions on a regular basis.

Stay in Your Lane

Roles and titles are very limiting the way we have traditionally seen them structured in corporations. Typically, they are about keeping employees (including leadership roles) in the box. This allows for supposed clear lines of delineation between responsibilities and work to avoid duplication. When it comes down to it, the way we interpret them is by boundaries and power. It's not a bad thing to have your job defined clearly and know the expectations of your role, but in this ever-changing business world, plus the long-needed change to the work culture, there should be "loose" boundaries. The opportunity is for reevaluation of what a role is and why a title is even needed. Most titles are not even representative of the actual responsibility and outcomes an employee is supposed to deliver. Also, as new structures shift from hierarchical to matrix organizations, titles become very stagnant and invalid. As customers require businesses to change how they serve them, it's important to create an agile organization and team who are empowered to make decisions to support that customer without having to run to their boss for approval or solutions.

There are a few thoughts on this topic of shifting to loose boundaries and outcome-based roles and how they align to the new work values expectations. I can't tell you how many times I've heard over the years as a peer, leader, and customer, "That's not my job." Really? Why is it not your job? Is it not your job to take care of a customer, do you just not know how to do the task required, are you lazy, are you fearful of someone getting upset that you took care of an issue, or are you not sure how to solve it? Yes, I believe all of these can be great excuses when employees are not empowered, enabled, or expected to support the outcomes the company has committed to. The main issue lies in rigidity and fear: rigidity in the process only being accessible to certain titles and fear that another employee or a manager will be upset if the employee takes the action needed. Sometimes employees are simply too busy or feel they carry the load while teammates are slacking. Of course, this is a real challenge of power struggles and fairness that management needs to address as a priority.

The work value of ownership is really important here because what is counterintuitive is the fact that the role has boundaries placed on it by management or by assumption, yet the expectation is ownership. What does ownership mean? Only take care of the specific tasks that role is required to do? Hand off professionally to someone who can solve the problem (no cold transfers!)? Or be empowered and enabled when something is outside of the employee's specific tasks? The way I would describe my expectations of ownership with my teams over the years includes creation (not just doing), problem-finding (not just solving), collaboration (not just with their team), development (skills plus experience) and leadership (regardless of title). Ownership means accountability for self, process, team, solution, service, and future evolution of the business practice. One of my favorite examples of empowering and enabling a team to establish an amazing culture was within the past decade. My leadership team had all different personalities, experiences, and backgrounds and were in the safe space of showing up as their authentic selves every day. This made things fun, but it also provided motivation and excitement for them in their roles. Since they were empowered and enabled, they led their teams that way.

How to shift a culture of doers to owners was a great challenge. The best part of this team was that we had grown so fast, and as the leader of the practice I could not be involved in every decision. The size, speed, and scale of the business also offered a ton of change within responsibilities on the team, allowing them to stretch and grow. So when someone would bring an idea forward, I'd respond with, "That sounds great, run it past your peers and implement it. Let me know how it goes." After a few rounds of this redirection of empowerment back to the employee, they just started doing it on their own. This created a culture of ownership, continuous improvement, and evolution at a speed that outpaced the company, which was all good because our customers benefited most. I loved how creative these folks were, and with the loose boundaries they expanded our practice significantly over the years. Many found new skills and gained different experiences they would not have otherwise been able to experience. Since they loved their jobs, they put a ton of passion and effort into creating significant impact.

One last thought on the opportunity for revolutionizing how we define roles and titles and align to work values: every company is different in how they approach career development and promotions. With the work value of always learning, part of the challenge is that typically an employee is told to take specific classes and sit with others to enhance their skills in their current role. It's more optimal to look at their true potential and enhancing their skills for other roles in the company that could be enticing. Authentic coaching brings forward the opportunity to define an effective development plan that incentivizes and excites the employee into putting the time into themselves and learning new skills. The workforce is changing rapidly and the shift to automation of tasks forces the need and opportunity to upskill teams. This should be part of the plan; companies have to develop their employees inclusive of an evaluation of all of the skills and talents their employees can bring to the table. Keeping in mind empowerment and enablement in this shift is key to avoiding resistance.

Make the Shift

Review how your role is defined and how you'd like to expand:

- Describe your role. (What is expected of you on a daily basis and what outcomes and value do you deliver?)
- Identify what you actually do that is "over and above or outside of" your role.
- Decide what else interests you or excites you to expand your knowledge, skills, and experience.
- Map out a game plan to discuss with your manager how you would like to shift some of your responsibilities to fill in gaps in process and creation.
- Get together with your team, if you are a manager and want to do a review, and whiteboard out expectations and what everyone actually enjoys doing. You are empowered to adjust who/how the work gets done. (I did this with a team in the past, and not only did the team members benefit, but the customer benefited by better SLAs (Service Level Agreements).

Keeping employees in the box creates a negative impact on what companies desire to deliver. Challenging the checkbox, roles, titles, and boundaries is a great first step to authentically revolutionizing the workplace.

4

HOW WE CLING TO IDENTITY

Without work, so much of one's identity just evaporates.
——Joshua Ferris

Who Are We in the Workplace?

Who we are can vary from home to work and everything in between. How we show up in the workplace brings a sense of identity to us and sometimes becomes a BIG part of our identity. We may be rock stars, high performers, overachievers, hard workers, or solid teammates. We may also be ambitious, approachable, articulate, calm, cheerful, dependable, intelligent, clever, autonomous, confident, collaborative, efficient, diligent, flexible, open-minded, opinionated, resourceful, controlling, persuasive, arrogant, bossy, defensive, confrontational, self-centered, cynical, thoughtless, inconsiderate, trustworthy, dishonest, vague, unpredictable, unreliable, and on and on. Of course, most of the negative characteristics above we don't typically accept about ourselves.

Interestingly, our perception of who we are in the workplace can actually be different than what others perceive of us. Our personal brand can change as we evolve, and perceptions of us can change as we do or say—or don't do or say—certain things in the work environment. Being authentic in the workplace brings forth an ease to flow and allows you to be yourself. There is a ton of energy spent trying to keep up an act or to figure out how others want you to be in order for them to accept you. Perceptions are what and how we see something and then maybe believe it, and they can be filled with assumptions versus facts.

I've seen people struggle so much with how they think they need to show up in the workplace that they end up becoming a tangled mess. They may even show up to one person or group differently than another. Most of the time this is due to perceived expectations of others and alignment to their brand. Every team inside of a company has its own collective personality, so those outside of the team feel pressure to approach it in a way that mirrors or matches that personality. What ends up happening is the individuals they may be working with don't feel they are being authentic or genuine and may not trust them. Now their perceived brand is marked or labeled. I could write an entire chapter on labels, but will not dive too deep. You can see the impact of labels sprinkled throughout this book.

The most important thing you can take away from this book is that showing up authentically can be one of the biggest impacts you can make on your business and others, and it is a key to happiness in the workplace. Giving permission to others to do so through showing up every day in this way is a gift. Overcoming limiting beliefs and narrow perspectives of yourself first allows you to be true to yourself. Your identity then becomes you—all in—versus someone else you may feel you have to mirror. Become an observer not only of yourself, but of others in a deeper way to see where you are able to recognize these gaps.

Make the Shift

Identify your personal brand through perceived and actual feedback:

1. Write down five things about how you think others would describe you and your work. (You can expand on this if you want to specifically go into collaboration, decision-making, or other topics.)

2. Ask five different colleagues to do the same exercise. (Tips: pick different engagement relationships such as leader, peer, support, etc., and pick people who are straight up and won't just tell you what you want to hear—you are looking for honest feedback.)

3. Compare your self-assessment to the peer-assessment results and answer the following:

    a. What are the similarities?

    b. What was shared in the peer assessment, but was nowhere on your radar?

    c. What are the gaps, and how can you bridge those gaps?

Next let's talk about what happens when we identify AS our job or company, since this is a real issue many of us have struggled with in our careers.

Identifying As Our Job or Company

What happens when that sneaky ego builds our identity around our work, title, role, or performance? Here's a quick quiz: how do you introduce yourself? Do you use your company name, title, years with the company, etc. in your response? Are you leaving the other part of you on the table? This is a real issue that many people have dealt with over the years. When we identify AS our job or company, this becomes the initial portrayal of ourselves. I realized a few years ago I was doing this even in nonwork functions, which was quite amusing. It was almost automatic. After finally realizing this, I started questioning why this was my introduction and not mother, community volunteer, or nature enthusiast. These were all an even bigger part of who I felt I was, but in reality, I had been so sucked into my work identity, then company identity (mainly due to being proud of being with a company for twenty-one years), it was all I spoke of in my introduction.

As I dug deeper into what seemed like a surface-level issue that I could easily change, I realized this was toxic. What I mean by toxic is this identity with my company was not in introduction only, it was embedded deeply through a cord—like an umbilical cord. It was my lifeline. As I started to peel back the onion, I realized that everything I based my day, goals, energy spend, and future on was tied to this company. I realized that I had become my company.

I mentioned early on that I worked with a psycho-spiritual healer and was doing energy work and past-life and current-life regression work. I had this planned list of topics I wanted to work on with each session (every two weeks). I just so happened to plan out a session on cutting the cord with my company (identity-wise) while I had vacation time. I was excited for this for months. As I was driving to meet my healer, I started thinking about what I had learned so far about this identity crisis and the deep roots that I had connected with over the years of working with this company. As I went deep into thought it occurred to me that day, January 3, was my twenty-year work anniversary. It was not at all planned and the fact that I even realized it was amazing. How appropriate that I was doing this healing session on my twentieth anniversary.

The thing about the cords we tie, whether to people, situations, or things, is that it's not as easy to just "cut" the cord and move on, especially when there is such a deep connection and tie to that entity. We worked through a cord-unraveling exercise, and as I went deep, I realized how hard it was to actually unravel my own identity from my company. I was a loyal soldier to the company and servant to my team and customers for so long, it felt like I was abandoning them. When we finished, I felt relief. That is the best way to describe it, almost like it was a last-ditch effort to regain myself—my true identity. The aftereffects of this went on for months while I was slowly regaining myself and balancing how much I gave of myself to my company.

Identifying with work is important, as it provides us with a sense of purpose, but when it becomes us, it is not a good thing. Here is how I explained this in an introduction I participated in during an interview recently.

I'm an INFJ-A, DI, ISTP, maverick, manifesting generator 2/4, sun in Aquarius, Moon in Taurus, rising Virgo, Sirius A, Avalonian. I'm also a Flo-grown native; married to my best friend, love, and wonderful partner, John; with five kids and two kitties.

Now, of course, there is a bit if sarcasm here to prove a point about changing up how I introduce myself. Those of you who are into personality tests, human design, and astrology will totally understand this intro and probably understand me better than any other introduction could have offered. It's pretty straightforward.

How does identity to a company, job, or title impact our authenticity? Given the fact that most of us work for someone else (company, boss, etc.), as we become our company or job we tend to do what is necessary to be effective and compliant. We rally for that company and want to see the best outcomes. This is a good thing except for me, where I saw the opportunity was in challenging the status quo. It's great for those of us who like to challenge the status quo of a process or offering; it typically provides innovation and advancement for the company. Those of us who challenge the status quo of leadership or culture may not be as accepted by the uppers. What became frustrating for me was the commitment to stay in the box (identity to company) and desire to break free and evolve our culture and company. Once I unraveled the cord it was much easier to support the evolution and revolution of culture shift and new ways of thinking, regardless of my loyalty to "the company."

Your work should add meaning to your life, but it should not be the "meaning of your life," even if it's the dream job you've always wanted.

Unraveling the cord does not mean you are no longer loyal to the company or job. It means you value yourself—your whole self, not just one component. It also provides the opportunity to feel less overwhelmed, set healthy boundaries, and speak your truth more often. For me, it was freeing. It allowed me to expand my curiosity into new areas of purpose and provide service in different ways. It led me down a new path.

Make the Shift

Craft a new introduction:

1. Review your answer at the beginning of this section (quiz). How do you introduce yourself? Do you have introductions in the workspace compared to outside?

2. Answer these questions: what is your own personal purpose? What lights you up?

3. Design a new introduction statement that is more encompassing of who you are (not just what you do). Maybe create one for the workspace and one for community/social.

Make the Shift

The five components to finding identity balance with work are:

1. Goals and priorities. Identify both short- and long-term goals (job and personal). What are your priorities, and which ones support achieving your goals?

2. Time and energy. How much time do you spend working (that includes cell/email time and THINKING time)? Do a check each day on your energy level at the beginning and end of the day.

3. Self-reflection. Are you neglecting your health for the sake of your passion project? Are you neglecting your family for the

sake of your new job? Instead of rushing to do more, take ten minutes each day to refocus.

4. Boundaries. Learn to say, "no thank you." Set a start and finish time for work each day (some days may be extra hours, but no more than once per week). No weekends or vacations, if possible. Set expectations on when you can get tasks or projects completed.

5. Laughter. One of the issues with "workism" is that we can become very serious. Find humor in your day, either with your teammates or laugh at yourself. This can break the chain of focus on our work identity.

Identity is much more than I've outlined in this chapter, since I was focused more on our identity in the workplace. But in diving deeper into these sections, I hope you find helpful information to bring awareness to your identity.

5

WHY EXPECTATIONS CAN BE PROBLEMS

An expectation is defined as "an eager anticipation for something to happen." A goal is defined as "a purpose or objective." When we are clinging to expectations, we are waiting for something to happen and giving our power away.
——Christine Hassler, *Expectation Hangover: Overcoming Disappointment in Work, Love, and Life*

Expectations of Self

In this chapter I'm diving into expectations. So often expectations become some sort of definition of what must happen. The relationship of expectation between two people or entities such as manager and employee or company and employee, of others in general, and of self can really become limiting. The conditioning that has been set for decades in corporations plus conditioning received growing up builds this mindset that we must deliver the best versus do our best or be our best. How we show up and the value we bring through our own authentic self is enough. Doing what we say we are going to do is enough. Supporting others genuinely is enough. Being available and present is enough. Let's focus on expectations of self and of others, because it becomes an outcome of expectations and fear that limits authenticity in the workplace.

I realize how expectations of myself over the years really took a toll not only on me, but I'm sure on others too. My motto is always excellence, but the quest to get there can be so unrealistic and daunting. Of course, this approach to excellence all the time can deliver an outcome that is not realistic to expectations or is over-delivered. I've always looked at opportunities as a sequence of phases and then looked to see how I can jump or skip some of those phases to "pull in" the outcome desired. I've found that while this can be innovative, efficient, and strategic, sometimes those around you aren't quite ready for it yet. The phases can actually be a good evolution of the opportunity. I think about the reason why pushing myself and setting high expectations was such a rhythm for me, and I believe it is tied to feeling the need to prove myself.

How many times do we approach a new challenge or opportunity with excitement that we get yet another chance to "prove ourselves," whether that is to prove to ourselves or to others? I think there is another reason many struggle with including themselves in certain special assignments or roles, and that is fear. When our families depend on us financially, we feel the need to prove our value in order to keep our job, and our teams are motivated by how they can add value to the vision, it becomes the pressure of fear of failure. Proving ourselves can be such a root for setting false expectations for self and others. It drives behaviors that may not be authentic or that are draining. Working eighty hours a week (been there) instead of designing and proposing a need to expand a team or to find new ways of supporting the business is not sustainable, nor is it valuable.

The belief that if we aren't valuable, delivering on targets, or effective in our strategy and leadership will lead to a stagnant career or losing our job puts a significant amount of pressure on us. In reality, we put most of the pressure on ourselves. The expectations we put on ourselves to avoid the fearful outcomes typically are much higher than what our bosses are expecting. Plus, this leads to over-delivering and creates higher expectations of others, which then leads to raising the bar on ourselves yet again. The cycle continues and before you know it, you're maxed out. Maxed out in time and energy spent, and this can become very unmotivating and exhausting.

Before you know it, you are pushing yourself to the limit and not showing up authentically. As I started to realize this over the past decade, I started setting boundaries for myself, asking for clarity of expectations of others and by providing very clear expectations I have of them. I found this gave relief not only to me, but to my team. The challenge becomes when you take on special assignments, projects, or roles on top of your day job. The last seven or so years in the tech industry were literally one special assignment or creation of a new department, team, or business after another. While the challenge to learn something new or create new teams and processes is enticing, using so much energy to try to balance those boundaries in a new environment can be very challenging. This is absolutely not sustainable. Instead, providing some normalcy between special assignments is ideal (i.e., just the day job). Otherwise, you can fall into yet again setting high expectations of self, especially if the outcome is not clearly defined because this is new to the company. It becomes the cycle of proving self and draining energy along the way.

I've found it much easier to stay within realistic expectations by giving/getting updates along the way versus trying to complete an entire plan, process, or proposal before sharing it to get feedback. This is really key to giving yourself a break on unrealistic expectations. It also gives you practice to share your ideas and approach, which provides confidence and the opportunity to share struggles you anticipate as you build. Of course, setting high expectations of self is not only an issue in the workplace, but also at home, in a certain identity you've associated with, and in public (social media, community, etc.).

We are a society of competition and comparison (we will dive deeper into these in another chapter), which drives high expectations of ourselves. This becomes a limitation to how we can truly show up in our fullest and most authentic way, sharing our struggles, being true to ourselves and to truth, and living our values through and through. The biggest way we can get sucked into setting unrealistic expectations of ourselves can be due to a carrot dangled in front of us creating desire and want. This can be a bad tactic used by those in companies, especially if it isn't realistic that it will happen.

Many times we may set unrealistic expectations of ourselves because we have been told to be like so-and-so, or we decide we want what they have (title, money, fame). This can go against being authentic. What if the way they achieved their goals is because they have different abilities than you do, and you put on a mask that only causes pressure to not screw up? What if the person did not follow their values to get the job, money, etc. they have, is that the role model you want to follow? It can be dangerous to use this tactic when trying to coach employees in a broad sense of competition, comparison, and carrots.

Make the Shift

Let's dive into an area of your personal life (if you don't have this issue in the workplace):

- Write down an area where you put high expectations on yourself.
- Ask yourself why you have set those high expectations. Is there a fear? Do you feel the need to prove yourself, is there a carrot being dangled, or are you feeling pressure to compete with others to keep/earn credibility or because you've always done it?
- Determine what is reality. Do a fact check and get feedback on what the actual expectations are.

- Find two to three ways you can align (set boundaries) with the true expectations and how to hold yourself accountable?

Now that we have looked at the expectations we set for ourselves, let's poke at our expectations of others. This opens up an entirely new issue and opportunity that creates limitations and impacts relationships.

Expectations of Others

Have you ever felt frustrated that someone wasn't doing, being, or saying the things you wanted them to? This is definitely much more visible in personal relationships, but what about in the workplace? A few years ago I read the book *Expectation Hangover: Overcoming Disappointment in work, Love, and Life* by Christine Hassler. It was a great book I highly recommend, and it opened my eyes to why we can sabotage so much in our mind by the expectations we set for others. Typically, we set an expectation, then don't communicate it, and when it doesn't happen we become disappointed. How does this impact authenticity in the workplace, and what impact does it have on others and on relationships?

Many times the expectations we have of others tends to reflect those we have of ourselves. I think we dove into that enough to see the challenges that causes. We may have expectations for a team and are limited in what we share with them of those expectations. Our expectations are probably unrealistic of them as a team and individually as well. One issue I faced when I first started managing people at age twenty-two was in that comparison issue. I would identify a "model" employee on my team and then expect everyone else to be like them. That didn't last long, because I realized it conflicted a lot with one of my values of fairness. What wasn't fair is that my team members ranged in age from seventeen to eighty-two years old and they had a wide range of experiences and goals. It wasn't possible for each person to mirror the best model. What I found is that as I started to manage each of them the way they received and accepted the best and found out what motivated them, I shifted my expectations to align with each of them.

I think one of the issues with expectations is we are not always consciously setting them. If we set aside time when starting a new role or with each new year, plan, or team and think through how we want to set expectations, we'd find it much easier to accept those that make sense, challenge those that do not, and be clear in communicating them. Hashing through expectations to validate the most impactful, realistic, and necessary ones saves so much grief and frustration in the long run.

Expectations are so critical in asking others to complete or create something. I found I had to be very specific up front when I'd request something like a report. Otherwise, they would work the weekend to get it done or prioritize it over something else, when it honestly was not necessary. I have had some folks on my teams in the past who had such high expectations of themselves that they would work late or on weekends to get the ask done. I started literally stating, "I don't need this until next Wednesday, and I hope you have the time starting Monday to work on it." I even said, "Please don't work the weekend." Or I'd say, "Based on what else you have on your plate, when can you get it to me?" So often, we assume our ask is realistic, but in that person's world it's just one task of many they are juggling to get done.

I've found stress caused by conflicting and ever-changing priorities is a daily opportunity to level set. One of the conversations I would have regularly with different teams over the years was: "What is causing you stress, what do you have on your plate, and how can I help to re-prioritize so you can reduce your stress?" I found this to be a great training as well to give them permission to be proactive in stating, "I have these five things due tomorrow. Can you help me determine what truly needs to be delivered tomorrow or is no longer a priority?" In fast-paced, high-energy environments, this process is necessary.

When people just suffer in silence, it can impact their authenticity. It's important to create a safe environment for employees to share their struggles and help them balance their own expectations with yours. This also goes for outside obligations including family, health, home, and community. I'll dive into perfectionism in the next section, which bleeds over from outside to inside the workplace.

I've had a few expectations I have set with my teams that end up becoming challenges because of their own expectations. That includes taking vacation and turning off email. I've even asked a few of my leaders to uninstall Outlook so they would not check email. I know not every position can totally disconnect, but in corporate environments where people are in masses, there is definitely a way to do this. People need to take a break, disconnect, focus on family/friends, and have fun without worrying about the next email. I've also had to be clear on expectations of after-hours emails. If I realized someone would respond to me regardless of time or day, I'd send an email I'd set for delayed delivery until working hours. Yes, I literally changed my way of communicating because I didn't want this person to feel obligated to respond at ten p.m. or on a Saturday. Or with others I'd just say, "Hey, when I'm in meetings all day, the only time I can get caught up or take action is after hours. I don't expect you to respond, it's just the way I need to work right now." Simply communicating clarity of expectations sets the tone.

It's funny, I hear from folks who have managers who wake up in the middle of the night and start sending a bunch of emails because they have stuff on their mind and literally can't sleep. The issue is that employees feel the need to check their email first thing upon opening their eyes. Then overwhelm hits them. It's a crazy cycle and SO UNNECESSARY. Responding to something an hour or two earlier than it could be handled during work hours is just insane. Leaders can make these changes and MUST.

I had a leader years ago who, starting on Sunday at three p.m., would send the brain dump, to-dos, and epiphanies. It totally ruined my Sunday! Not only was I still at the baseball fields, but I still had yet to go grocery shopping and cook dinner, make sure homework was done, and get kids ready for bed. The thing was, that leader did not find it OK to wait until Monday to respond. He expected a response within a couple of hours. Once he moved on and my new leader did not have the same approach, it was like I had half of a weekend back. It felt like freedom, yet it was my time anyway.

No more of this way of managing. NO MORE! Weekends are for family, friends, body, mind, and spirit and anything else we could not finish during the work week. Vacations are a benefit and needed (regularly). Period.

Make the Shift

For people managers, ask yourself these questions:
- How clear are you on expectations with your team (and individuals)?
- Do you create a safe space for your team to share when they are overwhelmed and need help re-prioritizing?
- Do you set expectations with your team to work within business hours or do you need to make some changes?
- Do you support your teams to take time off on vacation and weekends, and to support their family and health?

Make the Shift

For everyone, consider these approaches and questions:
1. Think of a time recently when you were disappointed in someone (work/home).
2. What caused you the most disappointment? How did you feel?

3. Was your expectation clearly stated before the action, behavior, or words happened?

4. If not, how could you have (a) challenged your own expectation, and (b) if valid, communicated it clearly to at least allow the person a chance to meet it?

5. What will you do today to identify a valid expectation you need to communicate to someone? Repeat daily.

6. Another approach is to focus on appreciation of a situation, person, or thing instead of expectations. It really shifts perspective.

6

JUDGMENT IS IN OUR EVERY DAY

The way out of judgment begins when you witness the judgment without more judgment.
——Gabby Bernstein, *Judgment Detox*

Judgment of Self

In this chapter I'm going to address judgment. Not only do we judge ourselves, but others, of course. Let's look at the definition of judgment by *Merriam-Webster:* "Judgment: the process of forming an opinion or evaluation by discerning_and comparing." Sounds reasonable right? We do this all day long. We leverage judgment in making decisions using inputs and assessing information. There are judgments passed down based on laws and rules. Yada. What I want to focus on here is this definition as it relates to how we judge ourselves and others—this part: forming an opinion or evaluation by discerning and comparing. Self-judgment in particular is defined as resulting from thoughts we have about ourselves and the meanings attached to those thoughts. Those thoughts can produce feelings such as anxiety, anger, or depression.

There are so many pieces of the puzzle that lead to thoughts of self-judgment including conditioning growing up (family, teachers, friends), expectations of ourselves, comparison (actual versus imagining what is supposed to be) and limiting beliefs. Typically, self-judgment is a mechanism we use to protect ourselves from rejection and failure.[4] There are both positive and negative self-judgments. Let's focus on the negative ones. We inaccurately believe that, "If I judge myself, then others won't judge me or reject me. I can be safe from others' judgment by judging myself first," or "If I judge myself, I can motivate myself to do things right and succeed. Then I will feel safe and be loved and accepted by others." The catch is that instead of truly motivating us, criticism tends to paralyze us, leading to no or slow action. And the cycle continues. It can actually become addictive. Thinking and believing things like:

I will always be poor, because I always have been. I'll never be good enough. I'll never do it right. I'm so stupid, I should have learned this by now. I can't believe this is happening to me again. I won't speak up because they won't listen to what I have to say. My boss doesn't think I'm capable, so I won't step up. I'm too (insert other random, harsh self-judgment here).

Some of the external criticism we have heard either while growing up, in toxic relationships, or in work environments can evolve into self-judgment.

The biggest thing I've seen is how "beating ourselves up" when we make a mistake or have an unforeseen failure can do more damage to our self-confidence and courage. This leads to not taking on new projects, not speaking up with new ideas or solutions, and even burying ourselves in spending too much time double-checking everything we do/write/create and trapped in procrastination. If it's a big deal that is lost based on a

---

[4] Margaret Paul , PhD. "Are You Addicted to Self-Judgment?" *HuffPost,*. January 2, 2018,. https://www.huffpost.com/entry/are-you-addicted-to-self-judgment_b_5a4be364e4b06cd2bd03e2d9

decision we made or our behavior, we can feel broken. We are not broken though, we are learning and growing. Breaking the habitual patterns of self-judgment can give us the shortcut to overcoming limitations we perpetuate for ourselves. We can improve productivity, confidence, sleep, and relationships.

An interesting personal observation I have on self-judgment, especially in the workplace over time, has been that as we are making the shift to humility in the workplace while still holding on to our credibility and proof of our ability, we have gone a bit overboard with self-judgment. I'm not sure if it's because we feel that is the definition and act of humility or if old conditioning is gaining more power over us. In the outcome of this shift we have the opportunity to balance how we act in humble ways without the self-sacrifice and criticism we have adopted along with it. Self-judgment has probably always been with us as part of our comparing self and is part of the ego's lifeline. It just has times in history where it tends to flare up more.

Self-compassion can be a great way to make the shift from self-judgment as well as a healthy practice that helps with many other limitations in our mindset. It's not selfish to be compassionate to ourselves and practicing it should also increase our compassion toward others. We will get into self-acceptance in part 3 of this book, which is such a critical integration step to embracing our authenticity and our gifts.

Make the Shift

A few considerations to shift self-judgment to healthy thoughts without judging them:[5]

- Awareness: What did I just tell myself that is causing this feeling?
    - Example: "I'm such a jerk, how could I have said that?"

[5] Gabrielle, Bernstein. "Judgment Detox: Release the Beliefs That Hold You Back from Living A Better Life", *Simon & Schuster*, October 9, 2018.

- Body: Where do you feel this self-judgment in your body?
  - Example: I typically feel a knot in my stomach.
- Truth: Is what I'm telling myself true? If not, what is the truth? Zoom out to assess the big picture as well.
- New thought: "Making a mistake does not mean you are a jerk, we are all human."
- Keep a count of how many judgments you think, hear, and see in a day.

Sometimes we struggle with self-judgment and sometimes we judge others. In this next section we will focus on judgment of others and the impacts it can have on authentic relationships in the workplace.

Judgment of Others

It's amazing how often in a day we judge not only ourselves, but others through our thoughts and words. It's also amazing how one person can create a "new belief" about someone else with a judgmental statement (not a factual one) that everyone else all of a sudden believes or at least considers. Judgment is not only dangerous to us as humans, but it's also damaging to our potential and can hold us back in all areas of life and relationships.

Not so long ago I was struggling with a couple of higher ranking people. Each in a different way, but both damaging to my confidence. As I worked through why this was becoming such a problem "all of a sudden" I realized they were playing out roles that I feared. Whether because they also played these roles in my past life/lives or societal conditioning, it was profound to me. I called them the judge and the executioner. The judge always had some specific comment (verdict) that made me feel I wasn't good enough or smart enough. The executioner was always trying to trash me behind my back (sentence). This sounds pretty hard-core, and it was. The biggest issue I had with all of this was that I had a good relationship with each of them in the past. Also, I don't recall ever having this dynamic in my previous career. It was all new to me and it was challenging to deal with it.

Here is how I found myself responding to these judgments. I started judging them. I would look for flaws and issues or even complain about their judgment of me. That spiral is not recommended to anyone. It was tough to break, but eventually I figured out a better way to deal with it. The best advice I received was "don't give them any attention." That came through in a meditation. Once I applied this approach, not only did their intensity stop, but I stopped as well. In the next section I'll go into projection, but as I realized much of their judgment on me was actually projection, it helped me to not take it so seriously. It was coming from a place of fear (theirs). They weren't afraid of me, they were afraid of the situation, lack of control and environment, but used it to judge and project onto me.

I'm not going to get into how damaging "gossiping" is in the workplace in this book, but that is typically a method used to share judgments of others to each other. I wanted to call it out here because as long as it becomes part of someone's behavior, it will spiral into a habit. Judgment works the same way. As we look at the world through a skeptical, glass half-empty mindset, we look for flaws in others and either use them to hurt those people or to make ourselves feel better about ourselves.

I've never gotten into office politics or water cooler conversations because I hate it. I'm making a strong statement on this because it's true. It actually turns me off from people who do it. I'm typically the last person in the office to know about something/someone because I distance myself so much from it. That was my approach for the majority of my career until the above situation happened. So I was able to actually experience what it's like to live a life without it, and then later dealing with and being a part of it. It's so not worth it!

I was the band captain and homecoming and prom queen in my high school. Not because I was anything special, but because I was friendly with everyone. I didn't judge them because they were in a certain clique or not. I went—and still go—out of my way to include those being excluded by others. I believe that kindness, acknowledgment, and compassion are key to living a happy life and probably the key to becoming united as a human race. I actually make myself feel bad for judging someone and quickly look for something good in them. I believe there is more good than not in everyone.

You've probably heard the saying, you never know what someone else is actually dealing with in their life. So don't judge (what I'll add on to that). In the workplace, judgments of others can keep you from building strong relationships, getting to know others, and being too harsh when it's so not necessary. If we feel judged, guess what happens? We don't show up as our authentic self. We go into defense mode or our ego tries to combat it with something not healthy. Judging others by how they dress/look, what kind of car they drive, how they communicate, how they lead, how they get their work done, how they handle a situation, where they live, what education level they have, what title they have, where they worked in the past, who they hang out with, who they support inside the company, or how many tattoos they have is just not going to be accepted anymore in the workplace. There is no cookie-cutter way to be anymore (the times of the standard for wearing suits everyday no longer exists) and people want to bring their authentic self into the workplace. Granted there are still dress codes, so I'm not saying to break those, but if you buy your clothes from a certain store because that is what your budget can handle, then so be it nobody has a right to say anything. Judgment on these grounds needs to stop to allow people to show up in other authentic ways. You will end up with a better team, more engaged colleagues, and more innovation.

There is a better way to live together, reduce our words/thoughts of judgment, and be more compassionate with each other. Judgment is a harsh world to live in, it uses up a lot of energy, and holds us back. It also hides underlying issues we could address and free ourselves from. Judgment definitely plays a role in holding us back from being our authentic selves limits our ability to grow, and impacts our relationships. Judgments may also be used against us in future decisions or performance reviews, so it is important to recognize this defense mechanism and work with it. Recognizing when someone else may be projecting onto us also helps to protect our own energy and feelings. Remember, always seek truth.

Make the Shift

How to reduce the judgment in your own mind/words and heal yourself from past judgments:

1. Realize when you are judging, but don't judge the judgment. Just acknowledge it.
2. Recognize when the judgment is tied to something you yourself struggle with.
3. Work through those challenges so you can move forward and not repeat the judgment.
4. View the big picture of the situation to shift your perspective about the judgment.
5. Release the connection to the judgment. Meditate, pray, or visualize cutting the cord.
6. Forgive what happened to you in the past and forgive yourself for the judgment.

As we slow down to recognize when we are judging, we will find opportunities to shift our thoughts to something positive and remove that judgment from future use.

7

HOW OUR MINDSET GETS INFLUENCED

The most important type of critical thinking directs itself inwardly to assess the trustworthiness of our own thoughts.
——Tara Swart, MD, PhD, *Author of The Source*

Limiting Beliefs

This chapter is a heavy-hitting chapter and one of the most important in terms of our subconscious superpower (or what could be our superpower). Mindset is one of our most important tools. Your mindset is a set of beliefs that shape how you make sense of the world and yourself. It influences how you think, feel, and behave in any given situation. It can seriously harm us and positively shape us. The great thing about mindset is we can change it. I fully believe this is one of the most impactful changes we can make in our life (daily) and continue to evolve. It's also one of the biggest things holding back so many people from living the life they desire.

Let's look at a few areas of how we acquired the mindset we have. Limiting beliefs are conditioned throughout our life through genetics, generational and ancestral beliefs passed down, karmic beliefs buried deep in our DNA from past lives, society, education, media, advertising, social media, family, and any influential person in our life (good or bad). Limiting beliefs hold power through fear and negativity. Comparison and unhealthy competition hold us back and can create a seriously negative impact on our mindset. A fixed mindset keeps us from expanding and can hold us into a pattern of stagnation and inflexibility. Plus we end up dealing with that fun old inner critic. The one that provides such great self-criticism (and also some good to help keep us alive). The brain and the mind are really two different things. We will focus on the mind in this chapter and explore all of these things that hold us back.

Have you ever challenged your own beliefs? In the sense of seeking if they are "true"? A belief is a thought we continue to believe. And we can change it. Beliefs aren't true, they're just real. All beliefs carry consequences with them and can create or destroy some of the most important areas of our life like relationships, career, and health.

There are two types of beliefs: global beliefs and rules. Global beliefs begin as "Life is ...," or " I am ...," or "People are ..." Rules are if/then statements that we create and tend to live by. The current brain is three thousand years old with a ton of old programming. The core foundations of our brain are in place to protect us and keep us alive. Fight, flight and freeze are the old built-in survival tools to help protect us in threatening situations. Today, instead of trying to save us from a tiger ready to pounce on us, it's using the same programming to protect us from modern threats caused by our limiting beliefs. However, our new "survival" level is all around awareness and about seeking alignment, purpose, our energy, and reconnection with our soul-self. These are very different times, yet we still fight, flee, or freeze when faced with today's "threat."

There once was a belief that the world is flat, so almost everyone accepted it. This held back societies from building sturdy ships and seeking new resources. Once Christopher Columbus debunked the belief, there was a new fact-based belief formed. The world is actually round. This is a simple example of how beliefs can be challenged and changed to truth or simply something else. We have become a culture of theory and opinions, so most everything including watching a sporting game is narrated by personal observation and based on that narrator's beliefs.

Those beliefs can infiltrate our minds and become our truth IF we allow them to. It's important to seek truth instead of just accepting. Come up with your own perspective and attitude toward something. The biggest challenge we are up against is the infiltration of so much information that has bias with it. How many times have you found yourself parroting information you heard this morning or read on social media? I'm guilty of it too. As you state it out loud (especially to someone), is it stated as a belief or as an opinion? What we speak can become a belief or at least what someone else thinks is our belief.

When we identify those beliefs that are limiting us in achieving what we are seeking, we completely hold ourselves back. This goes for individuals, family/friend groups, and company and team cultures. Clarity, regular and effective communication, and myth-busting are great ways for managers to help teams overcome limiting beliefs, especially in a time of great challenge or transition within a company or industry. When we bring our limiting beliefs about our self-worth, ability, intelligence, execution, and effectiveness to the workplace, they completely hold us back and keep us from fully enjoying the learning and growth process in our career. I've spoken with so many people who struggle with "imposter or poser syndrome," held back by money beliefs and confidence.

Think about how performance reviews and grades in school and on standardized tests and how they typically highlight our inefficiencies or deficiencies. What limiting beliefs have they formed for you that you still live by? Which ones are holding you back? Of course, measurement is a great way to push ourselves to expand, improve, and grow, so I'm not saying "measurement" is a bad thing. It's how the measurement is delivered to us. Is it a made-up comparison and set of standards created by someone, or a group, or is it PFA (or pulled from ass)? Or is it some high set of standards to try to raise everyone up? Unfortunately, the negative impact that can cause can be long-lasting and truly impact other areas of a person's life besides just intelligence and performance.

Some examples of potential limiting beliefs on relationships include:

- I will never find true love.
- This won't last.
- They should treat me how I treat them.

Some examples of potential limiting beliefs on money include:

- Rich people are mean.
- There is not enough money.
- I must get what I want, how I want, when I want.

Some examples of potential limiting beliefs on health include:

- I just can't lose weight.
- I don't have time.

Some examples of potential limiting beliefs on self-worth include:

- I am not good enough.
- I don't deserve (fill in the blank).
- I must/should always do well and win the approval of others.

Some examples of potential limiting beliefs on ability include:

- I am not an expert.
- I'm an imposter.

Limiting beliefs don't sit in a box and hang out separated from other limiting beliefs, they merge and blend and grow. Eventually, they infiltrate our entire mindset in many areas of our life.

There are many negative consequences of limiting beliefs impacting your scarcity, "not good enough," definitive (always/never), abstract (could/should), tribal betrayal, and relevance mindsets. Scarcity thinking could be around money, love, time, food, others limiting how much you receive or give in a relationship, your actual money situation, and time limiting what activities you bring into your day for fulfillment. Feeling not good enough or smart enough and other self-worth limiting beliefs can cause hesitation in going for your dreams, taking action toward goals, self-care and love. It can also cause depression and unwanted solitude.

Having limiting beliefs that are definitive and using words like always and never will keep you from driving toward your goals and meeting fantastic people in your life. Abstract, limiting beliefs and using words like "should" and "could" keeps things out of grasp around you without ever solidifying results.

Then there are limiting beliefs in place because we don't want to betray our family or friends (tribal) that can keep us from succeeding in our career or unhealthy because that is what the tribe believes and does. Limiting beliefs around relevance and depending on significance and validation can slow down your decision-making process and cause perfectionism, allowing the ego to drive your day. Victim and blaming mindsets require a conscious responsibility for where you are and deciding what you want to change.

Think of failure as feedback. Instead of creating or attaching to new limiting beliefs when failure happens, shift your mindset from failure to feedback to help you improve, shift, or gain momentum in a different way. Awareness is key to ensuring you don't continue to add to your library of limiting beliefs. Seeking truth is another great tool to add to your analysis of your beliefs, as well as getting the brain to acknowledge the evidence, which will show it that the original intent of protecting the limiting beliefs has actually held us back. The last one is, just let a thought enter your mind, acknowledge it, and release it instead of locking it in as a belief. Think of it as simply information.

The stories we tell ourselves are not only influenced by experiences in the past and present, but of future expectations and fears. The hierarchy of fears for most people is:

- I won't be myself.
- I'll get rejected.
- I'll be humiliated.

- I'll feel invaded.
- I won't exist (death or vacancy).

Living to our true identity is our biggest desire, so when we are not authentic, it can cause us suffering. In the workplace, we may tell ourselves that we will "never" become an executive, or make over $200,000, or that the only way we can make more money is through working an eight a.m. to five .p.m. job, overtime, and promotions. Our limiting belief started our journey and our stories keep us on that same journey. Tony Robbins says, "Change your mind, change your life." And I would add, change your story. Things are changing and shifting from old paradigms and ways of thinking and doing. Now is the time to truly challenge all of the old stories and limiting beliefs that partner up with the old ways and look for a new way of being, doing, and achieving your desires.

I mentioned in the introduction to this chapter that genetics can actually impact our limiting beliefs. Epigenetics has discovered that historically, our lineage inherited suppressed genes during severe stress. For instance, if your great- or great-great-grandparents lived during the depression and went without food in severe circumstances, the need to avoid wasting food, clean your plate, or scarcity thinking can literally be carried in your genes. Mainstream science only knows where about 12 percent of DNA actually comes from. There are so many hidden, limiting beliefs that we don't even recognize are holding us back. Even those buried in our DNA. Let's change them.

I'll end this section with something that will not only blow your mind, but your brain. I know I mentioned I was only going to focus on the mind here, but there is so much discovery that has not made it to mainstream about how our brains work, challenging beliefs that science has it all figured out. While we have been told for decades that the brain is pretty much set by age seven, research has now determined that for those of us in the 25–65 age range, we can do things to change how our brain sees the world. We can apply certain lifestyle changes to support shifting limiting beliefs. We can literally grow our brain! This process is called neuroplasticity. There is a great amount of research published, and I touch on this a bit at the end of part 2, but Google it. You will be amazed, and it will open up your belief that there is so much more yet to be discovered.

Let's become more conscious about the stories we tell ourselves. When we do, we can change those stories to truth. When we become aware of what is our truth and what is not, it provides us an easier way to challenge beliefs that pop up. It shifts the approach to seeking the truth of them versus just believing them. When we change our mindset, we become intentional about what we create in the non-physical and physical worlds.

Make the Shift

Let's use some quantum linguistics to shift a belief by creating new neural pathways. Use this method for challenging limiting beliefs and embedding new beliefs.

1. Create a belief you wish you had and move it to a fact. Set up the truth of this belief and simply embed it in your brain. You can state the belief multiple times to make this happen.

2. Journal on a problem. Say to yourself, "What wouldn't happen if I didn't have this problem?" (Some examples include worry, self-shame, burnout, overwhelm, holding back, etc.)

3. Simply challenge limiting beliefs using critical thinking. Ask yourself:
   a. Is this the truth?
   b. When has this not happened?
   c. Do the facts support this?

Comparison and Competition

There are four Cs that I believe can break a company culture and business: competitiveness, comparison, compliance, and complacency. Let's talk about comparison and competition here, and I'll dive into compliance and complacency in a future chapter. I'm going to take these separately, but they do intertwine and can both have the same negative outcomes or impacts to our mindset.

In a world where we are basically encouraged to compare ourselves to each other or to famous or "successful" people through social media, titles, income, looks, and our bodies, it's no wonder we tend to feel shameful or not good enough more often than not. The silent yet in-your-face pictures, articles, and features flooding our information highway can create a sense of personal comparison, even if we don't realize it's happening. It's brought on more consumerism and accumulation than ever, and it has had impacts on our own self-worth. I'll get to the inner critic in a section coming up, but beating ourselves up because we are not good enough is one of the most harmful impacts to our mindset.

The typical underlying message is that we are broken, our home is not up to par, we are behind, and we need to step up in society and our culture. Even further, from a parenting perspective we need to do all, be all for our children and keep up with what other parents are doing or supporting for their children. Otherwise, we are just not good parents. This includes the schools/programs our children are participating in, the grades they receive, the college they get into, what we allow our children to do (screen time, accountability), and their behavior. As we head into the workplace, comparison and competition can have an even greater negative impact on each of us, the team, and culture.

Competition in the workplace can create motivation, upskilling, and even fun. Encouraged the wrong way, it can create a shameful, unmotivating, and resentful environment. I used to think that sending out group kudos emails or recognizing to others the folks doing an outstanding job was a great way to create some healthy competition. It's a pretty easy formula; you are aware as a leader and create a process to recognize folks for something unique or a specific situation where they stepped up to help a customer, etc. It can work if done in a fair and consistent way. When it causes a negative outcome is when it's the same people all the time, only the "big" deals are recognized, or it's done to drive competition. Recognition is something that we all crave and have been conditioned to believe we will have if we go above and beyond. What really happens is not all leaders are created equal and they do not have a consistent practice of appreciation for their team or aren't close enough to members to be able to highlight the great work they are doing. What happens when recognition repeatedly doesn't come? Low confidence. Resentment, not only toward the leader for not recognizing them, but if there are certain folks being recognized over and over, resentment toward them as well.

When we come from a scarcity mindset, we tend to compete with each other. Typically, women in particular have struggled with the number of opportunities in higher-level positions. When a scarcity mindset is present and the view that opportunities are slim pickings, it becomes about competing with each other. On the other hand, men typically have a competitive mindset.

Competition in the workplace also creates resentment when promotions occur for the same people over and over. In performance reviews leaders say, "Hey, why don't you look at how so-and-so is doing their job and model them as part of your development plan?" This is great advice as long as it's done in a way that does not shame them for not being enough, but instead calls out very specific items or skills to model. Modeling is a fantastic way to cut through the shit and time it may have taken someone else to figure out how to master something. I highly recommend it. It's just a tactic that needs some care in delivering. How competition and comparison become visible can be in these tactics in the workplace. As we start to compete, what are the main things we ask ourselves? What title or job is that person doing? How long have they been in that position? How many hours are they working? What kind of recognition are they getting? Who is sponsoring them? What "club" do they belong to? What certifications do they have? What special projects are they working on?

Competition can come out unhealthily when we shift our intention from good to selfish, and when we compete with someone or others because we want more money or to get recognition. I've seen people trash others just to make themselves look better. Ugh, very selfish. When a culture of competition goes off the rails, it can be extremely difficult to change. Leaders all the way up need to own the culture and model healthy behaviors for their teams to be and grow in a healthy environment. The person we should be competing and comparing ourselves with is ourselves. How do we make ourselves a better person then we are today? Collaboration doesn't happen when unhealthy competition is out of control. The infamous CYA (cover your ass), lack of trust, protection of ideas, and lack of self-confidence on teams become the foundation for engagement in unhealthy competition. A healthy competitive environment has boundaries and expectations where respect and appreciation for others is above all else. Collaboration over competition is the shift we need to make in corporate environments and leaders should be expected to lead by example. A culture where members can be their authentic self allows for growth, innovation, and creativity to blossom individually and as a team.

Comparison is a heavy, low-vibrational energy, but it can be healthy if we recognize it's happening and truly determine if it's helpful or not. Sometimes, it can help motivate us to get up off our butts and do something that we've wanted to, and now that Suzie is doing it, we feel motivated to as well. It can also motivate us to lean into our strengths and focus on making those central to our lives. If it's not healthy, we can break it and shift our thoughts and beliefs. Being authentic in every way allows for us to be in gratitude and appreciation for what we have and who we are. Evaluating our standards, upgrading them when needed, and awareness when we are straying away from them is key. Breaking the chains of induced comparison is such a freeing feeling. Living with intention and in our values and beliefs allows for a healthy comparison if it motivates us.

Make the Shift

Recognize whether you are in comparison and how you can make the shift out of it.

1. Awareness in and of itself is a super-helpful way to break the chains. Setting your own personal and professional goals that align with your values and beliefs and sticking to them with integrity can help keep the silent hacker from getting in.

2. Choosing to take a different path if you do recognize comparison, whether with your intentions (switch to a good one), pausing your mind to get real (breathe), and acknowledging your feelings (anger, pain, shame, sadness, resentment). Acting with scorn and contempt toward others can have other serious consequences that you may not be able to reverse.

3. If you find that certain things trigger you like social media, PTA parents (that was one of mine), media, certain leaders, colleagues, or even organization announcements, remove them from your day. Don't look at them, read them, or think about them. Let them go.

4. Shift your mindset through your state. Go for a walk, dance, or, if at work, throw on some music in your headphones to change your state. Get into what you are grateful for and focus on what that means to you and to your goals and desires.

8

WHAT YOU SAY TO YOURSELF MATTERS

It's not what you say out of your mouth that determines your life; it's what you whisper to yourself that has the most power.
——Robert Klyosaki

Self-Talk

Self-talk is a natural way we assess information and use our internal representations. When it's positive, it's fantastic. We can work through decisions and solutions, and pump ourselves up to be courageous. One of my favorite representations is provided in a blog on Healthline.com:

> Self-talk is *your internal dialogue.* It's influenced by your subconscious mind, and it reveals your thoughts, beliefs, questions, and ideas. Self-talk can be both negative and positive. It can be encouraging, and it can be distressing. Much of your self-talk depends on your personality.[6]

The thing is that self-talk is not always positive and encouraging. It can be negative as well. Negative self-talk can be limiting and even

---

[6] Nick Wignall, "10 Types of Negative Self-Talk (and How to Correct Them),". *Nick Wignall July 27, 2018*, https://nickwignall.com/negative-self-talk/

dangerous. What we say to ourselves impacts our self-esteem, behavior and even decisions.

I'd like to poke at negative self-talk and how it impacts our authenticity in the workplace. We have explored expectations of self, judgment of self, limiting beliefs, comparison, and competition. You can see where I'm going with this, I'm sure. These are all contributing external influences on what fuels our negative self-talk. They bring in the opportunity to basically tell ourselves that we are not good enough.

I'm going to also emphasize how assumptions tend to fuel our negative self-talk. For example:

- Assuming someone is not responding to you because they are upset with you or don't value you, versus that they are working feverishly on a deadline and not looking at email.
- Assuming someone got a promotion because they are better then you, versus they took on extra projects to gain extra visibility for this promotion.
- Assuming you were not asked to take on a project because you won't be effective, versus your manager seeing how much work you have taken on and trying to respect your time and energy commitment.

When we look at the things we say to ourselves, we should first ask if this is something you would say to your child, parent, or best friend. Probably not. We can be super-harsh on ourselves, yet we would never say these things to others. We should then challenge the truth of what we are saying to ourselves. Is what we are telling ourselves true? Probably not, so just don't believe it!

Self-talk can definitely impact our self-esteem and confidence. It can shape how we show up—authentically or not. If you are not sure about something, either ask for clarification or just wait until it comes up. Try not to fill in the blank. Leave it be until the answer(s) come forward.

Don't beat yourself up for not "knowing," since we aren't supposed to know everything.

Make the Shift

How to determine if it's healthy or unhealthy self-talk:

1. Listen to what you are saying to yourself. Ask yourself, "Is this helping me to move forward or holding me back?"
2. *Challenge* it. Has this ever been true? When has the opposite been true? Would I say this if it was about a friend? If the response is a much more positive and healthy thought, then go with that.
3. Determine if this running commentary is repeating itself in a loop. Break the chain. Think of something totally different. See if it just goes away or replace it with something more healthy.
4. Shift the words you are using to healthier ones.

Let's finish up this chapter with a dive into our inner critic. I call mine Fred (sorry to those named Fred out there, it's just an easy name that gets my attention). You notice I personalized my inner critic. This is a great tool to help reduce the influence your inner critic has on your mindset. Let's dive in.

Fred, My Inner Critic

Why did I say that? That was stupid. I'm not smart enough to figure that out. Crap, what did I do now? They don't find this presentation interesting. He must be upset with me for something. I'll never get offered a promotion. I should just look for a new job. I never fit in. I'm such an idiot. Why didn't I just be patient? There's no way he's going to call me again. I'm a loser. Why am I so clumsy? I'm a fraud. The harder I try, the worse it gets. Just give up. I screwed up. If I speak my mind, they'll think I'm a bitch. I am a failure. I'm not meant to win and succeed. I'm not enough. I need to make sure I know what I'm talking about before I open my mouth. Nobody cares what I have to say. Suck it up and quit bitching. Don't be lazy, I can always do more. Good moms don't get frustrated this easily. Other people don't care about me. I'll always fail. It doesn't matter how hard I tried. What I'm doing won't work. It's my fault.

Meet Fred, my inner critic. He's short and stocky and has a whiny voice. He's a know-it-all and really freaking annoying. He likes to cut me off and will just keep digging in and digging in. This is how he gets my attention, and why I no longer take him so seriously. These are some of the things he used to (and still tries to) say to me pretty much daily. He's the one who pops in whenever there is space to analyze, build on, or create a situation that may or may not be true. He has held me back from going after promotions, and damaged my confidence in myself on new projects and in assuming what others think of me. Yep, he's a bugger. I try to get along with him, but I've found I have to really set boundaries and pay attention to what he's going on and on about. I've also learned to create nonthinking space to give it all a break.

What is an inner critic? According to Wikipedia (it's not referenced in traditional dictionaries) the inner critic or "critical inner voice" is a concept used in popular psychology and psychotherapy to refer to a sub-personality that judges and demeans a person. The inner critic is that part of the mind that identifies problems, flaws, and mistakes. The inner critic works to erode your confidence and take away your belief in yourself and your capabilities. It wants to make you live in a perpetual state of fear, doubt, worry, and anxiety. It can enjoy antagonizing or bullying you when it all comes down to it. Is what the inner critic says real? Heck no! Our subconscious mind is here to protect and preserve us and does not know how to translate information. This gives us a great opportunity to change how our inner critic works and what it "says."

Negative self-talk impacts our authenticity, particularly in the workplace. When Fred starts in on me about not being good enough, not smart enough, or needing validation from others, I used to just believe him. It was me telling myself these things, right? Oh and they were true, right? It's amazing how our inner critic can really damage our self-esteem and confidence to do the things we desire and achieve our goals. It can literally keep us from taking chances, going after the things we want, and from being our true self. In the workplace, it can cause mistrust with others and impact relationships by the assumptions we make. It can also keep us from speaking up, when we tell ourselves what we have to say isn't important. The protection our subconscious is trying to enact through our inner critic can end up keeping us from what we want to pursue, say, do, or be. There is also a risk of blaming and finger-pointing based on this inner critic's whispers.

There are different types of negative self-talk.

Mind reading is when we fill in the blanks to a situation by assuming we can read the other person's mind and know what they are thinking. "She must be upset with me for something".

Overgeneralization is when we use words like always/never in situations which bring more emphasis to them in our minds. "I'll never get offered a promotion; I should start looking for a new job."

Magnification is when we take a mistake we may have made and exaggerate it. "Great, I'm sure that will end up in my annual review."

Minimization is when we belittle the effort we may have made as not a big deal. "It was nothing."

Emotional reasoning is when we make decisions based on what we feel instead of what we value. "I don't want to invest in that stock, I'm afraid it's too risky."

Black and white thinking is using extreme categories in our thoughts. "I'm such an idiot."

Personalization is when we just burden ourselves with criticism. "I'm so clumsy, why can't I be graceful?"

Fortune-telling is a big one that keeps us assuming we already know the negative outcome of what others will think or do. "That wasn't very good, there's no way that customer is going to buy from me."

Labeling is very common, using descriptors in an oversimplified way. "He's such a jerk."

Should statements are when we try to motivate ourselves to make decisions with more certainty then we have. "I should have known this deal was not going to close."

Keep in mind that limiting beliefs end up coming into play here, too, so if we can do the work on shifting our beliefs, it has a positive impact on how much and what kind of role our inner critic plays. How we can use our inner critic effectively is really key and will help in being in our authentic skin. Look for valid reasoning as, typically, the inner critic is irrational. This shift alone can help you make decisions you would not have made otherwise based on the whispers. Talk to others and get a different perspective, as they will see things differently. Your closest board members may know your struggle with imposter syndrome or confidence in your job or achieving goals, and when you share your thoughts, they can help identify if the thoughts fall into the limiting belief you are struggling with. I think it's important to state here that learning to trust your gut/intuition can also help minimize the whispers.

Make the Shift

So how do we get a handle on our inner critic and slow down the conversation going on in our mind?

- Make it tangible. Give your inner critic a name, avatar (description), a voice/tone, attitude, and anything that will help you recognize it when it rears its head. If the voice or tone you choose is compassionate and kind, it's easier to just let it go. If, like me, you respond better to being annoyed by your inner voice, then use that tactic (give it a name of someone who reminds you of your inner critic).

- Choose to believe in yourself. When your inner critic starts to get loud, use this phrase to break the crazy chatter: "I believe in me!"

- Silent third-person self-talk. This is proven to be very useful in regulating emotions and improving self-control. Instead of using the first approach above, you can instead use third-person pronouns (you, he, she, it) or your own name (first, last) in your internal conversations. This disassociation approach also activates the vagus nerve and reduces the "fight-or-flight" sympathetic nervous system responses according to Christopher Bergland's research and *Psychology Today*.[7]

- Validate your feelings. Instead of analyzing them, just observe and notice these feelings instead of trying to solve for them. Keep the brain from thinking this "feeling" is a problem.

- Be still and quiet. Meditate often to help train yourself to get to this state. Breathing techniques help as well. Slowing down tells our brain that we don't need to "fill" space with endless chatter.

- Journal. Writing about the situation like you are a reporter outside of your body and mind can help with creating space to observe the thoughts and acknowledge the feelings as if they belong to someone else.

- Use positive affirmations. These are a great way to get in phrases that can help shift this negative inner talk. I started using affirmations about five years ago, and they have made a

[7] Christopher, Bergland, "Self-Talk Using Third-Person Pronouns Hacks Your Vagus Nerve" *Psychology Today.* May 23, 2017. https://www.psychologytoday.com/us/blog/the-athletes-way/201705/self-talk-using-third-person-pronouns-hacks-your-vagus-nerve

big difference for me. Affirmations are so much more than just words of encouragement or emotional support—they have the ability to completely change our perspectives of ourselves and our circumstances. At the end of the day, affirmations are statements we tell ourselves over and over again that affect how we feel about ourselves. Try it. Get started with these and create your own. Put them somewhere you can access them easily and say them throughout the day (post-it, index card, phone/computer home screen, or notes).

- o I achieve my desired outcome through focus and determination.
- o My time will come, but my coworker's success is also my success.
- o I am calm and confident.
- o I have all the skills and knowledge to deliver at my dream job.
- o I always speak with confidence.
- o My job brings me joy and happiness.
- o I am confident in my self-worth.
- o I allow myself to grow and learn.

9

WE DON'T NEED DISTRACTIONS

Focus on a specific intention ... A goal is often fueled by fear ... An intention is fueled by a sense of purpose.
——Robert G. Allen

Overwhelm—the "Big O"

In this chapter I'm going to share how distractions in the workplace can impact our ability to fully show up with all of our gifts as our authentic self. I'd like to focus on three specific impacts and outcomes of distraction including overwhelm—the "Big O"— multi-tasking insanity, and escapism. Nearly every person I've worked with over the years struggles with any or all of these areas. As I've been building out the challenges we have as individuals and as organizations that hold us back, managing distractions can be a breakthrough.

Overwhelm is an experience that impacts so many of us in both work and home life. It's caused when we believe the stressors we are dealing with are far too great to manage, and we become overwhelmed. I'm going to focus mostly on work-induced overwhelm. Expectations, to-do lists, and the many increasing tasks we put on ourselves grow and grow until at some point we are just overwhelmed. Now repeat this every cycle— whatever that cycle might be. Most companies plan from a quarterly perspective and then break it down to monthly goals. Employees with children also align with their kid's school cycle—beginning of school year, insane paperwork barrage—then to the season of projects due, typically right before Thanksgiving, and exams before winter break. Repeat most of this again in the spring plus add in sports, dance, scouts, church, or other activities. Even if you don't have children, you have other outside cycles to contend with including tax season preparation, renewing licenses, family expectations and other repeat activities that may or may not overlap with the intensity of peaks in the work cycle.

Not only do these cycles create the cycles of overwhelm, especially when they all come together, but lack of sleep, emotional state, and poor nutrition reduce our ability to be able to handle the increased responsibility. I myself have yet to figure out a solid exercise or body movement routine that keeps me committed, but know many others who absolutely need this and commit to it in order to manage the peaks and avoid the feeling of overwhelm. More and more the need to stop, breathe, meditate, take a break, and move our bodies is critical. How can we break the chain of needing to always be *doing* and just *be* for ten minutes? This is why I included the "Big O" under distractions.

Distractions are what we create or allow based on expectations we believe exist, programming that we need to be productive, guilt if we slow down or attempt to take care of ourselves, and comparison of our life to others that creates a competition to do more. These distractions we create may or may not be necessary, yet they exist, and when we pile them on we hit overwhelm. Then there are the uncontrollable situations and issues that happen. Layer those onto the mix and you have a recipe for overwhelm. Then we dive into distractions even more to escape from reality. Every year it seems that more and more is piling on us in and outside of work with pressure to be more productive and increased hours of work. There is naturally less of a boundary between work hours and nonwork hours, and our phones keep us connected to work always. It's becoming clear we need to move away from distractions in order to keep our overwhelm down.

In the workplace, there is pressure to increase our income through a promotion and on a time line we establish based on our perceived or actual needs or expectations. When we are in the mode of trying to prove ourselves, we look to "fill space" with anything that makes us look productive and/or busy, even if it's not necessary to get the outcomes or hit the goals. We sign up to take on projects we really don't have time to do. We create specific spreadsheets to track every little thing we are doing or focused on so we stay in control. Then we expect ourselves to update them regularly and, more than likely, manually. We set up meetings to discuss topics that can probably be done in email, or we take on the work of others to "help" the team. When it comes down to it, we use these tools as distractions. They take us away from making the difficult phone call, or having a difficult conversation with someone who is struggling, finalizing a tough decision, closing the deal or facing someone we do not want to talk to.

When we build on distractions through modes of activity and tasks we pile onto ourselves, there are so many expectations that, when just one more thing comes in from a manager or customer, we become overwhelmed. We hit the "Big O." This is typically the signal that it's time to clear out some of what's on your plate, but instead we take on more rather than asking for a lifeline. Then we complain about how much is on our plate, over and over to everyone who wants to listen, thinking maybe it will go away. It doesn't until you make changes, ask for help, say no, or re-prioritize what you have. I love the approach used in transformation and aligning priorities to strategy, and that is asking ourselves what we stop doing, what we start doing, and what we keep doing. This can be applied at the individual level. What can you pause or stop doing until you get your head above water? Maybe something you start doing is saying, "no thank you!"

Overwhelm has become such a significant impact on not only our authenticity and ability to have the time and space to connect with all of our gifts, but also on our health. When stress increases so significantly that we become overwhelmed, it causes a cycle of other physical and mental health impacts. When you begin to feel overwhelmed, cortisol surges through your body and leaves you overloaded with intense anxiety. At the same time, our serotonin stores, the chemical that helps our bodies fight off depression and anxiety, start to deplete. This combination causes the intense feeling of total despair associated with being overwhelmed. It's really important we figure out a solution for overwhelm, especially as it's happening in faster cycles that will end up burning us out.

Make the Shift

Here are some suggestions to reduce overwhelm. As you start to evaluate your overwhelm cycles and make some changes, continue to look for other ways as well.

- Acknowledge your thoughts and emotions. Try to identify what you are feeling and thinking. Much of the anxiety created in overwhelm can be challenged. Reverse your thoughts and work through uncomfortable feelings. Identify which of these are future-based. Those that are created and not factual are much easier to reverse.

- Add in your daily breathing and meditation techniques that help to ground your energy and anchor you in the present.

- Take inventory of everything you are doing in a day. What is truly expected and what have you created in order to be productive and prove yourself? Remove what is not truly necessary.

- Determine how you can use your resources. What can be outsourced or delegated? Ask for help.

- Say "no thank you" to anything that you do not have the capacity to take on.

- Learn your cycles so you can break them. Try to spread out any new projects that don't peak in time and energy needed when work goals are expected to be delivered.

- Work with your manager or a coach or therapist if you are experiencing extreme overwhelm. There are so many techniques that can help empower and enable you to reduce repeat cycles of overwhelm by getting to the root cause.

Multitasking Insanity

I used to think that multitasking was a gift. I am a great multitasker, because I can focus intently. It's my superpower. I'm so productive when I do so much in a day. Well, after doing it so crazily and for so many decades, I finally realized it's exhausting and does not allow for full intention and attention. Results may be great or half-assed. What I didn't realize for a long time is this approach is draining and impacts not being able to fully engage all of my gifts. When I would take the time to fully immerse in a new idea, strategy, or solution to a problem, I was able to utilize the gifts that would bring those to reality. This is because several studies have shown that high multitaskers experience greater problems focusing on important and complicated tasks, memory impairment of new subject matter, difficulty learning new material, and increased stress levels.

What is multitasking by definition? It is performing two or more tasks at the same time, switching back and forth from one thing to another, or performing a number of tasks in rapid succession. Shifting the mind all day long from one task to the next actually goes against its natural desire to keep things simple and preserve the body. And studies show that switching from one task to the next takes a serious toll on productivity by as much as 40 percent. Multitaskers have more trouble tuning out distractions than people who focus on one task at a time. Doing so many things at once can actually impair cognitive ability. While our subconscious mind is processing at least 134 bits per second of information, our conscious mind can only take in about 7 +/- 2 pieces of information. The brain is not meant to multitask.

Switching from one task to another makes it difficult to tune out distractions and can cause mental blocks that can slow you down. I found this was even more so when my responsibilities spread across many different parts of the business. Switching context all day, whether it was calls, meetings, creating, or conversations with team members for each of those areas was exhausting. There are some tasks that we are robotic about and can do with our eyes closed and without thought, but with so much information coming in visually and audibly, it can be overwhelming.

This is because in the brain, multitasking is managed by executive functions. These control and manage cognitive processes and determine how, when, and in what order certain tasks are performed. According to Meyer, Evans, and Rubinstein,[8] there are two stages to the executive control process, (1) goal shifting: deciding to do one thing instead of another, and (2) role activation: changing from the rules for the previous task to rules for the new task.

Part of the issue of multitasking is the start of the day when we pick up our phones after opening our eyes for the first time. Our minds start going and we start feeling the pressure to get everything done that we need to do. New to-dos start overriding the plan we created the night before, and we lose control before the day even starts. Another area is meetings or video calls. This is not a new issue due to remote working, but it already existed in physical group meetings too. Laptop open, email open, and guess what's going on? Half-listening while looking at email, creating documents, booking travel, or other tasks needing the brain. After leaving a meeting where critical information was shared, I've repeatedly seen

[8] J.S. Rubinstein, D.E. Meyer, J. E. Evans, "Executive control of cognitive processes in task switching" *Journal of Experimental Psychology: Human Perception and Performance, 27*(4), 2001: 763–797, https://doi.apa.org/doi/10.1037/0096-1523.27.4.763

someone start asking, "So what's going on with this program (or issue)?" If they would have just listened in the meeting and avoided the other distractions, they would be fully informed. Instead, it was obvious they were not listening. This can create major disconnects, especially in a very fast-paced environment.

When we look at the impact multitasking has on decisions, it's also clear that the brain gets fatigued and it becomes challenging to make the best decisions. If we are distracted, we take in half of the information. If we are tired, we can't process it well. If we are overwhelmed, we shortchange the potential impact of our abilities and our gifts.

Over the past few years I've backed way off from multitasking due to the context shifting I was having to make with back-to-back calls and meetings. Some things I just cut out and some things I pushed off. What I found is that I was more focused and attentive to that particular topic or task and was able to be more effective and productive in getting whatever work done around it. This also allowed me to strengthen my other gifts like bringing in new ideas, planning more holistically into the future, and more strategically outline effective plans.

Make the Shift

To become more productive through less multitasking insanity:
- Use the "twenty-minute rule" and stick to each task for at least twenty minutes before shifting.
- Limit the number of things you juggle at any given time to two.
- Invest time into prioritizing and re-prioritizing so you don't feel the pressure to do it all at once.
- Take a quick assessment of the various things you are trying to accomplish if you catch yourself multitasking and need to be productive..
- Eliminate distractions and try to focus on one task at a time. This includes allocating time slots in the day for email review

rather than constantly looking at it. Turn off your notifications.

- Create more structure in your work by performing highly creative tasks in the morning, and then take a short break before moving on to each different task.

10

PUSHING OURSELVES OVER THE EDGE

Escapism isn't good or bad of itself. What is important is what you are escaping from and where you are escaping to.
——Terry Pratchett

The Escape into Escapism

Let's talk about escapism. The combined definition of escapism is the tendency to seek distraction and relief from unpleasant realities, especially by seeking entertainment or engaging in fantasy. So that doesn't sound so bad, does it? It's not as long as you go back to Terry Pratchett's quote above. It depends on what you are escaping from and where you are escaping to. I wanted to talk about escapism, and while it's a bit different then "numbing out," it is still something that can become a negative if you are struggling with work. Numbing is a coping mechanism to mask emotional struggles or trauma, whereas escapism is simply the opportunity to escape reality.

I love reading books, and this is one of my escapisms. I also enjoy diving into a Netflix show. Here is where it can get a little overboard. I would come home from work and want to veg (of course after everyone else and dinner were taken care of). This was my cue to my hubby that my brain

Love Your Gifts

needed a break more than anything. I needed a break from making decisions and a break from the realities of the day. I have found having a glass of wine enhances this escape, which is fine, but when it becomes a habit almost every day, it's time to question why.

There are many impacts a workday can cause that bring on the need to escape reality. Mostly it is about routine and the mundane. It can also be about the lack of feeling the ability to be our authentic self. When we struggle to be in our true skin for nine to twelve hours a day, that reality is not where we want to be. Of course we would want to escape it. That doesn't even include the increased energy we use when we are not our authentic self, which causes exhaustion.

When life gets overwhelming and everything seems to fall on you, it can cause you to want to escape it. The easy ways to escape are TV/Netflix, alcohol, a good book, social media scrolling, and a bubble bath (highly recommended). What I've found is there are some other really great ways to escape and enhance not only your brain, but energy. So why would you want to enhance your brain if you just want to veg? It's a different approach to what your brain has been working on all day (which is similar to yesterday and will be similar to tomorrow). This is a tactic that many genius inventors and creators have used over the centuries. Find something you know nothing about and dive in. Take a class, pick a book to learn from versus just consume, read articles, watch documentaries, or play a board game.

I've found balancing this form of escapism with the typical way provides not only a way for your brain to shift, but your energy grows with the excitement of learning something new. It's not about knowing more than others or being the smart one in the room because you explore other topics, it's about shifting what your brain processes. It also becomes a question of boredom and the need to always be consuming information. Give yourself permission to disconnect from your phone, sit still, and take in your surroundings.

82

Our bodies are where we tend to hold much of our day as well. Finding something that interests you to move your body helps to move stagnant energy versus just sitting (especially if you have a desk job). This could be dancing (check out ecstatic dancing on YouTube—it's amazing), walking/biking, yoga, stretching, exercising, gardening, and cooking. It is important to listen to our body and when it says, "I'm tired, I need to rest," do it. Self-care is critical and making the time for you (versus scrolling social media) helps to reduce how much escaping is needed.

Distractions and escapism are a great way to avoid the underlying issue. This could be overwhelm, crazy tasking, authenticity issues, emotional distress, or other stress-related challenges. Instead, let's figure out new ways to work through our underlying struggles using less distraction and a more thoughtful approach on making the changes that support a more balanced mindset and mind/body connection.

Make the Shift

Here are five ways to reduce the need to escape:

1. Think about how you showed up to work today. Were there areas where you were not your authentic self? How can you make a shift to be your authentic self?
2. Determine how much energy you spent in your workday on tasks, decisions, and plans that you could have delegated.
3. Identify how much of your task, decision, and planning fatigue carried over to before and after work. What can you delegate, outsource, or ask for help in sharing responsibility?
4. Find three topics you have been interested in or you would be willing to dive into. Take one to two of your escapism nights a week and dive in, reducing the number of nights it's Netflix or consuming alcohol.

5.   Investigate ways to move your body. Instead of escaping to the typical, consider taking a yoga class (or video), dancing with your kids/self/dog or significant other, or going for a walk.

On Ultimate Burnout

Since we are energy and we use our energy, it is important to manage our energy use. Protecting our energy from draining negativity is one way to manage it. Awareness of the types of habits that drain our energy can allow us to make a shift to protect it. The ultimate state of pushing through every day expending more energy than we have is burnout. This has become more common, and the cycles of burnout for each of us are spinning faster and faster without as much time to recoup in between cycles. Most of it is caused by our desire to achieve our goals (at a faster rate), the myth about productivity, and taking on way too much in our day-to-day activities. This leads to stress to get more done, which can impact our mental health and lead to burnout. When this happens, it actually puts us further from our goals. Burnout also impacts our personality, authenticity, and relationships. When we are running on fumes, we have less patience and ability to make decisions, and more poorly plan our time.

Let's hit on achievement again, as this can be one of our own personal drivers that leads us to burnout—even more so than anyone else's expectations of what we do, how we do it, or when we do it. Striving for achievement is a good thing, it helps keep us motivated and can help us accomplish our goals and find personal growth. When it's not a good friend is when it drives us to burnout. Setting realistic expectations and goals for ourselves with ideal timelines is key, then squashing assumptions we may have about what is expected or what we think will be accomplished (get the facts). It's important to balance our need to prove ourselves with that of achieving goals. If achievement is driving or motivating us with the underlying need to prove ourselves or please people, it's not healthy. Dig in deep to switch that storyline you are telling yourself.

Let's tackle the myth about productivity. I've now lumped this in with the "P" words that lead to burnout. Working more hours does not mean you are productive. Working late at night and early in the morning does not mean you will be successful. Somehow there was this expectation that more than likely came from the box that started pushing us to extend our workday and work twice as hard for the same pay. Yep, something else we can change.

On the note of productivity, it has become almost a fear-based tool leveraged by the box people to push for more. Is it the right thing to do? Heck no. They are totally missing the point. It's time to do a check on "how" work is being done. With automation, more skills, and software tools available, we can actually be more productive. So why are we doing double the tasks with the same old methods? Why are we double-checking each other's work and why do we need repeat meetings when a solution was already identified? We have taken productivity and changed it to being busy. It's not efficient with more output in less time. It's more time spent to get work done. That's not productive. It's time to reframe expectations around productivity, challenge the status quo, question industry standards (holding us back), and redefine how the work gets done.

What are those everyday habits that can drain our energy, especially in the workplace? Taking things personally, making assumptions, setting unrealistic goals, over-stressing, fueling drama, complaining all the time, overthinking, gossiping, multitasking, always checking email, always checking the phone, and trying to please others. When we spend our energy on these areas unnecessarily, we use up a precious resource that could be used to achieve our goals more effectively, build stronger relationships, and end the work day with a lot more energy left for self and family. Having a more fulfilling day brings a sense of balance and helps to avoid the need to escape.

Setting priorities on the surface level seems to be an easy activity and skill. I call it a skill because I've seen prioritization being done all over the map! The other "P" word that impacts prioritization is procrastination. How you look at what you need to do, who needs it, and by when is a great place to start, but how much of that do you really want to do, truly understand how it needs to be done, and feel confident enough to complete it? This is where procrastination can impact prioritization. The three key drivers of procrastination are fear of failure, lack of clear instruction, and lack of interest. A great way to determine how to prioritize what's on your plate is to use a simple four-box approach to grouping items (versus a linear to-do list). There is an extra step in thought to determine where the item should be categorized. Determining if it's something you actually like doing, or not, and something you're good at, or not. Place your items based on this setup, and then mark the items that are urgent with a star.

- Top left: Good at and favorite thing to do
- Top right: Good at and enjoy doing
- Bottom left: Good at and don't like
- Bottom right: Not good at and don't like

Mark those not a priority with an X and draw a line through anything in the bottom quadrants with intention to offload or trade out. Find a partner who is good at or likes doing this task. Do a swap with them, if possible, or simply delegate. Anything with an X can go on another list (parking lot); don't let it distract you. Looking at things based on how you can make an impact and enjoy them will reduce procrastination while you are prioritizing and executing activities.

When I finished my manuscript and originally focused on this section there was a key piece I was missing. Of all of the sections in this book at the time I asked my twenty-five-year-old son to review this section to get a perspective of someone early in career. He too worked in the Tech industry for the past couple of years and started his MBA program last year. When he shared his thoughts he said, "Mom I related so much with this because this is exactly how I feel, burned out". Although work had been pretty crazy with remote and many people leaving his team, increased business, etc. this was not the first time he dealt with burnout. While in college, he started his own business, an EDM production company. He recruited new artists (DJ's and live art artists), negotiated contracts, planned production operations, provided input on marketing and influenced investors (for almost every show which were mostly weekly or at least every other week). Plus he was a full-time student at University of South Florida-St. Petersburg as an economics major and worked a bar back position out on the beach where he ran his butt off.

What was interesting, looking back at how fast-paced he lived his life, is even though he knew how to handle it, he had not had enough experience building resilience to it. You can see the capability, energy, passion, prioritization and organization he had. What he didn't have was resilience. Not yet. Knowing how to set boundaries, saying no, letting go of something until he had more time and energy or how to recover were just starting to blossom. So when it became a constant thing it was just overwhelming. Burnout happens to each of us mainly because of much of the above, but also because we don't recognize when things are getting to be too much or we have too much on our plate. We just do what we need to do. I also think with Covid we have been limited with looking ahead to fun and things that help us recover from burnout that maybe we traditionally were able to do.

Boundaries are a big part of burnout as well, and most people in the workplace hesitate to set them because they feel the pressure to be in the box with everyone else. I've dedicated an entire section to boundaries in the workplace in a few chapters, but wanted to touch on them here. Boundaries can help to bring control into your day and energy, including how you handle drama controls, pushy people looking for answers right now, and expectations of the workday and how you spend it. Boundaries are not only good for you, but also for others so they understand clear expectations and have the opportunity to honor them.

I want to talk more about time off and vacation time. One of the main reasons we burn out is we feel like, if we just keep pushing and can get to X date, everything will ease up and we can breathe. Or, if I can just get through this week, I can rest on the weekend. Unfortunately, the lines just keep getting blurred more and more, and the more you do, the more you are expected to do. This has created no down time in between the crazy work cycles, causing more rapid burnout. You do have a choice in saying no to taking on more work, extending deadline agreements, and taking time off. Block your calendar way ahead of time (in out-of-office mode), and set expectations that you will not be able to join calls (delegate someone else or ask for meetings to be moved to when you are available). Enough is enough! Take your vacation and take time off regularly in alignment with when you need it before burnout can happen.

I've seen very skilled people re-prioritize daily to ensure they are not getting overwhelmed, setting aside enough time to complete tasks, communicating expectations pro-actively, and providing updates well before expected deadlines. I've seen many people do a great job managing time off and setting expectations ahead of time with their team and manager that they won't be available—truly disconnecting and leading by example. The more often you do this, the more productive, refreshed, and balanced you are in the workplace.

Make the Shift

Check-in with your burnout:

1. Mark on your calendar how often you are getting to burnout (which months and at what times?).

2. Look back over the last year and count how many days you took off from work (vacation, time at home, etc.). Was it spaced out, or did you have to go for long stretches in between time off?

3. Determine how that compares to how much time you are benefited to take off. Right now, start planning a time-off strategy over the next year. Use the information in step 1 to figure out how often you should schedule time off.

4. Note how you are prioritizing your to-dos and how much you are taking on. Work the quadrant sample above to see what you can delegate.

5. Find the underlying root cause when you get to burnout. Are you taking on more than you can handle with crazy hours or energy spend?

6. Check in with your expectations. Are most of the deadlines you wish to accomplish self-inflicted? Do you have control over resetting them to be more realistic?

7. Be aware of your habits. What habits are draining you and how will you make changes?

8. Start thinking about what boundaries will help you manage your energy and reduce burnout.

11

WHY OUR ENERGY IS SO IMPORTANT

Recognizing where our energy is dispersed is key to healing any "problem"
area we may have.
——Dr. Sue Morter *from* The Energy Codes

We Are Energy

In this chapter we will dive into our energy. Energy is something we loosely throw around as an accessory to living our day-to-day. We have had limited exposure to how we can better manage our energy and use it to better flow in our life. Why? Because we are energy. Managing how much energy you use through the course of the day to stay somewhat balanced is a great start to being aware of your energy. There are times our energy is low and others where our energy is lit up. Years ago I started learning about how EMF radiation (electromagnetic frequencies) impacts our energy. Things like our TV, computer, cell phone, microwave, and even vacuum cleaners can give off EMF radiation. There are many impacts, but the one that ends up being very obvious is the energy drain we feel. The following sections will dive deeper into the energy system running through us, burnout, and protecting our energy. I'm a firm believer that if we don't make the changes to keep a healthy energy system, it impacts other areas of our being including showing up as our authentic self.

In a pursuit to better understand how to find "balance" and better manage the energy I was spending, I was led to learning about our chakra system. In Sanskrit, the word "chakra" means "disk" or "wheel" and refers to the energy centers in your body. These wheels or disks of spinning energy each correspond to certain nerve bundles and major organs. Each chakra works to help keep our body in balance and thereby promote physical and emotional well-being.

As I've been learning about our chakra system over the past few years, I realize how much our chakras are impacted by our work self. When we are not in alignment with our authentic self, we are also not aligned in our chakra system. How I started to tune into this connection was in understanding what each chakra represents and what happens when it's blocked or imbalanced. I found this awareness helped me significantly to not just suffer with something "bothering" me and would go to work figuring it out. When I was struggling with a relationship at work, I felt it in my heart space (tightening, anxious energy). When I was struggling in speaking my truth or made a bad decision, I felt it in my throat chakra (tightness or illness). When I was struggling with fear of losing money or my job, I'd feel it in my root chakra (ungrounded). When I was struggling with overwhelm, I felt it in my sacral chakra (numbness). When I was struggling with tapping into my intuition, I felt it in my third eye chakra (blocked, stubbornness, and lack of "big picture"). The most impacted (besides my root) was my solar plexus. Typically, my issue was depleting my solar plexus energy through overworking, giving away my personal power, and doing versus being.

Our chakras cannot function at their best when there is a blockage or imbalance in the energy pathway. Common causes that reduce a smooth energy flow through our chakras include physical blockage or imbalance (nutrition/exercise/exertion), emotional or psychological blockage or imbalance (anxiety/depression/addiction), or spiritual blockage or imbalance (internal/external restrictions). Knowing this means we can go deeper into our energy system to identify those needing to be cleared and those needing to be opened. We can have an imbalance or blockages in one, a couple, or all of our chakras at the same time. It's important to be able to tune into the feelings we feel when we have an imbalance, blockage, or issue causing us some kind of physical cue that we need to clear a chakra.

It will be good to have a quick summary of what each chakra offers us. For purposes of this connection to how our chakras play a big part in how we show up to work, I'll focus on the popular seven chakras: root, sacral, solar plexus, heart, throat, third eye, and crown. For anyone not familiar with our chakras, I'll illustrate a summary of each chakra including its color (for visual folks), location in the body, and value when clear and open. If you are interested in learning more about chakras or working with a yoga studio to dive deeper into your awareness, I highly recommend it. I also have a bonus chakra-clearing guided meditation available at www.angiemccourt.com/loveyourgifts. What is amazing is that, as ancient healing technologies have been or are being rediscovered and brought back to people, there is even more evolution of how many people practice connecting to their chakra system. Some believe that well over one hundred chakras exist, and that the meridian system (ancient Chinese) and other modalities also combine to bring the most amazing healing technologies to us now. Here we go on the chakras.

1. *Root chakra* is represented by the color red and is located at the base of the spine. Overall it represents instinct and survival. When it is balanced, you will feel, do, and see the following: fearlessness, increased capacity for love, stability, a solid foundation, a stable career, a sense of belonging, self-preservation, trust, security, financial security, status in the group, survival, grounding, independence, stillness, and focus.

2. *Sacral chakra* is represented by the color orange and is located a couple of inches below the belly button. Overall it represents emotions. When it is balanced, you will feel, do, and see the following: less complaining, more appreciation, joy, play, better relationships, creativity, flexibility, outgoingness, creative risks, self-evaluation, an improved circulatory system, originality, and increased activity.

3. *Solar plexus chakra* is represented by the color yellow and is located just below the rib cage. Overall it represents energy. When it is balanced, you will feel, do, and see the following: increased energy, less watching and more doing, courage, self-esteem, developed sense of self or self-identity, vitality, ability to say no, expression of ego, purpose, personal power, self-compassion, self-respect, improved nervous system, better willpower, and confidence.

4. *Heart chakra* is represented by the color green (or pink) and is located across your chest (not only over your physical heart). I like to call this heart space. Overall, it represents love. When it is balanced, you will feel, do, and see the following: love, less judgement, more acceptance, compassion, gratitude, self-acceptance, increased ability to say YES, self-knowledge, and forgiveness.

5. *Throat chakra* is represented by the color turquoise and is located at your throat (including jaw, chin, upper neck, back of neck). Overall it represents truth. When it is balanced you will feel, do, and see the following: less talk, more listening, better choices, self-expression, improved communication, knowledge, wisdom, honesty, articulation, real vision, and good decisions.

6. *Third eye chakra* is represented by the color indigo blue and is located at the center of your forehead between your brows.

Overall, it represents intuition. When it is balanced, you will feel, do, and see the following: less frowning, more smiling, reason, insight, intuition, discernment, concentration, receptiveness to advice, focus, determination, and curiosity.

7. *Crown chakra* is represented by the color violet or white and is located just above the top of your head. Overall, it represents connection. When it is balanced, you will feel, do, and see the following: less thinking, more feeling, oneness, spirituality, divine wisdom, understanding, selfless service, awareness, self-realization, and self-empowerment.

Make the Shift

This is a visualization exercise to get connected to your chakras. Read the instruction and then close your eyes to visualize for each one until you feel comfortable flowing from chakra to chakra in your mind.

1. Visualize a red disc or sphere spinning at the base of your spine.
2. Visualize an orange disc or sphere spinning just below your belly button.
3. Visualize a yellow disc or sphere spinning just below your rib cage.
4. Visualize a green disc or sphere spinning in your heart space.
5. Visualize a turquoise disc or sphere spinning in your throat.
6. Visualize an indigo blue disc or sphere spinning between your brows.
7. Visualize a violet or white disc or sphere spinning just above your head.

The lower chakras affect our well-being and our ability to relate to our self and society (root, sacral, solar plexus). The upper chakras affect how we connect with the outside world (throat, third eye, crown). If one or more chakras spins too quickly, we feel hyper, tense, or overly nervous, causing us to feel burned out. Or, if any of our chakras are spinning too slowly, we feel tired, ungrounded, and lacking creative energy. So what happens when our chakras become blocked or imbalanced? Next let's look at what happens and how it impacts us in the workplace, our business, and authenticity.

Clear the Blocks

Energy is all around us and that includes the spaces where we sleep, live, eat, work, and play. Have you ever walked into a room and felt the energy of the room, or just walked into an old house? They all hold energy, give off energy, and receive our energy. We can tell when energy feels good and when it feels bad or negative. In this section I'm going to walk through what can happen when our chakras are unbalanced or blocked and how it impacts the workplace, business, and each other.

1. *Root chakra,* when out of balance, blocked, or has residue, can cause a sense of being overly fearful about security and survival. It can lead to feeling ungrounded, flighty, tied down, restless, or generally fearful; having poor health, difficulty letting go, or a feeling of not belonging anywhere; or being habitual. We can be overly practical and lacking in imagination. We will stress about money and financial security.

    Work issues can arise when one or more people in the workplace have a root chakra that is out of balance, which can include not being connected to what customers really need and are struggling with, fear of losing a job or client, lack of ability to rally the troops, a reduced team effort, and job dissatisfaction.

2. *Sacral chakra,* when out of balance or blocked, can cause us to feel emotionally cold, emotionally overwhelmed, hyperemotional, not good enough, and emotionally numb. We experience difficulty changing, struggle with experiencing joy,

have guilt, and low energy. It holds us back and can create a constant fear of betrayal.

Work issues that can arise when one or more people in the workplace have a sacral chakra that is out of balance can cause emotions to run all over the place (too much or not enough). There can be a lack of change management, lack of trust, and lack of empowerment. We can see challenged relationships, stagnation in new ideas, and feeling fearful of sharing ideas.

3. *Solar plexus chakra,* when out of balance or blocked, can cause us to feel a lack of confidence, low self-esteem, powerless, shame, a disconnection to goals, and a constant fear of rejection. We may misuse power, have an over-inflated ego, show dominance, have an overreliance on will, or play victim. We can have an inability to commit and follow through on goals, and an unrelenting inner critic.

Work issues that can arise when one or more people in the workplace have a solar plexus chakra that is out of balance include low self-esteem, poor branding, or a lack of execution and achievement of goals. It can fester micromanagement, lack of servant leadership, authoritarian decision-making, and power struggles. There can be reduced enablement, accountability, and commitment.

4. *Heart chakra,* when out of balance or blocked, can create a lack of compassion, unhealthy relationships, and feeling less than others. It can also lead to people-pleasing, over-loving (suffocating), jealousy, and constant fear of being alone—even in the workplace.

Work issues that can arise when one or more people in the workplace have a heart chakra that is out of balance include no bonding amongst work groups, unhealthy relationships, codependency on manager or other teammates, a culture of entitlement, judgment, jealousy, and gossip. Grudges against colleagues and too much people-pleasing limit effectiveness.

5. *Throat chakra,* when out of balance or blocked, can cause an inability to communicate ideas, problems with self-expression (expressions of own truth), inconsistent communication, feelings of low-value, a constant fear of being out of control, problems with creativity, manipulation, deceit of self or others, and lies.

   Work issues that can arise when one or more people in the workplace have a throat chakra that is out of balance include dysfunctional communication, a lack of trust, out-of-control deception, failure of employees to bring ideas forward and speak up about injustices, group think overwhelm, and manipulation of not only people, but also of systems, goals, and processes.

6. *Third eye chakra,* when out of balance or blocked, can cause a lack of imagination and vision, reduced concentration, clouded or misuse of intuition, distorted vision, illusion, becoming overly-reliant on logic and intellect, inability to see the "big picture," strong moodiness, and stubbornness.

   Work issues that can arise when one or more people in the workplace have a third eye chakra that is out of balance can show up as malfunctioning intuition, inability to see the "big picture," withheld vision, lack of inspiration, slow decision-making, too many assumptions, overanalyzing, missing out on bigger opportunities, and lack of focus on the work at hand (which slows things down). Stubbornness leads to lack of inclusiveness and new ideas. The illusion that everything is working just fine is a big one that can cause so many issues down the road with the business, customers, and employees.

7. *Crown chakra,* when out of balance or blocked, can lead to feeling ungrounded, indecisive, impractical, difficulty with finishing things, rapid thoughts, obsessive thinking, and analysis paralysis. It can also lead to loneliness, confusion, feelings of meaninglessness, constant fear of alienation, lack of common sense, grandiose ideas, delusion, and ego attachment.

    Work issues that can arise when one or more people in the workplace has a crown chakra that is out of balance include feeling lonelier and disconnected from employees, the higher up you go in a company; slow decision-making, confusing messages (such as with priorities), being overly attached to achievements, and inability to see others' points of view.

One way to help remove collective blockages and imbalances and help each person have a space that works with their chakras is in the actual workspace. This can be done through using the colors of the chakras in designated spaces as well as some specific spaces for each chakra that can be considered or incorporated into the workplace.

The root chakra can relate to the entryway of an office space or building—think reception area. It is important to provide a safe, welcoming, grounded feeling where either guests or employees can catch their breath as they enter.

The sacral chakra aligns to our circulatory system, so the office space pathways or hallways should flow easily and fluidly with some emotional connection through artwork or positive sayings.

The solar plexus chakra relates to the technology (center) or individual workspace using technology, but it needs to be connected to others. It cannot be an overwhelming energy, or it can be detrimental to the group.

The heart chakra aligns nicely with an eating area and any other potential social area. Social events getting employees away from their work to engage each other in nonwork fun is a great way to create a space to support heart chakra energy.

The throat chakra relates to conference rooms, video calls, and any space where truth and ideas are given a voice. I also like to think that the new types of collaborative spaces where there is a safe place for teams to brainstorm can be an even more impactful solution. This is a more nonjudgmental and cooperative space than conference rooms tend to be.

The third eye chakra can be supported by a meditative or quiet space. If that is not available, create a ten-minute break at a workspace with uninterrupted time, or go for a quick walk.

The crown chakra relates to a visual connection to the outside including messages about who the company is, why it exists, and the part its employees play in making that happen. This chakra connects the workplace to a sense of higher good in key areas.

The more we tune into how energy impacts us, the better we can find balance, happiness, and embody and align to the world within and around us.

Make the Shift

Are your chakra(s) blocked or unbalanced? Reflect on the following questions to assess your chakras. These are very limited for the sake of space, but check out more information available via Google, including chakra assessments.

1. Root: do you feel you are resourceful and prepared when you face challenges in your life?
2. Sacral: do you experience joy from your work relationships (colleagues, customers)?
3. Solar plexus: how do you respond when you receive criticism from others?
4. Heart: do you feel accepting of yourself?

5. Throat: do you feel a lack of connection with any specific purpose in your life?

6. Third eye: would you describe yourself as a highly skeptical person?

7. Crown: are you regularly bored? Are you obsessed with material items?

To learn how to balance or open your chakras go to www.angiemccourt.com/loveyourgifts to download your bonus Chakra Clearing Guided meditation.

12

WHAT HOLDS US BACK

Complexity is the enemy of execution.
——Tony Robbins

Compliance and Complacency

Compliance is a very valid consideration in the workplace to reduce risks and keep things safe, ethical, and legal for colleagues. The definition of compliant as an adjective according to the *Oxford English Dictionary* is "inclined to agree with others or obey rules, especially to an excessive degree; acquiescent." Dictionary.com provides its definition as "complying; obeying, obliging, or yielding, especially in a submissive way." Macmillandictionary.com states "too willing to do what other people want or too willing to accept their opinions."

I'd like to address the side of being compliant as it relates to how people behave when fear or control plague the culture of a team or organization—where the situation causes employees to feel helpless, resentful, and stagnant. In some organizations or by some leaders, compliance is a goal—kind of like that old box trick. Keeping everyone doing the same things makes it easier to "manage" or control them. In reality, it does damage in achieving goals, growing a business, personal growth of skills, and innovation. Productivity, creative solutions, motivation, and the quality of customer service are impacted as well. The end result becomes disengagement and even resentment toward the leader and/or company. Micromanagement, calling out mistakes (especially publicly), fear-induced motivation, silos and one-way communication are key indicators that compliance culture prevails.

Being compliant also reduces the ability for colleagues to be authentic, bring ideas forward, and trust. They lose their personal power. It also creates complacency. There are two types of complacency I've seen in cultures. One is robotic, and the other is the "badge of honor." Complacency defined: self-satisfaction especially when accompanied by unawareness of actual deficiencies.

Complacency in regard to the robot is all about "mindless" repetition over rewarding challenge. Doing the same job for ten years does not mean you have ten years of experience doing that job or task. It means the first year was learning and the next nine years were repeating it. When we feel complacent in a role or inside of a company that does not allow for challenge and learning (or does not expect it), complacency can become a foundation. It's easier, less risky, and uses less energy. It's also less fulfilling. We are less engaged with the vision. I have seen very committed and loyal folks also be complacent for reasons such as just wanting to keep things simple or not considering their job the key area where they want to put their energy during the course of a day. The danger is complacency leading to compliance and shrinking our impact and big-picture view.

Complacency can also be covered up by the badge of honor. Filling up our calendar does not mean we are productive. Doing tasks that don't add value and just take up time in the day is not effective. Bragging about the amount of hours we work or how much we don't sleep at night is not a valid badge of honor. It's a problem. Productivity does not mean working twenty-four hours a day. This goes for feeling pressure to get up at five a.m. every morning. Kudos to those who do, but it's not an expectation, nor right, for everyone.

I used to work with these two women a couple of decades ago. They were always in the office very early and stayed late. They lived close to the office, whereas I had a one-and-a-half-hour commute each way and a toddler, daycare, etc. I always felt like I wasn't doing enough because they were at the office before and after hours. One had older children and the other did not have any yet. As the pressure and guilt rose, I started second-guessing my value and commitment to my job. Then I took a step back. I started to really notice how often they were chatting in the hallway (at least two hours a day), out to lunch (I ate at my desk) and how much work they were completing (the same as me). I realized that some people just feel the need to be at the office, showing their "dedication" physically. It did not mean I was any less committed. It did teach me about complacency versus using time and energy toward rewarding challenge.

The last two of the Six Human Needs are *growth and contribution*. These are not critical needs, but essential ones. They offer fulfillment, not just survival. These are needs that are at your core, yet many never really focus on them in their effort to find fulfillment. One of my biggest bits of advice mentoring many colleagues over the years was to not stick to their "day job." What I mean is, mastering the job responsibilities in your role is great, but only sticking to those will probably not get you on the path you are looking for in career advancement and fulfillment. Find rewarding challenges and ask for them. Being the right-hand person to a manager/leader representing an organization is a great opportunity to gain visibility, but being empowered and enabled to make decisions on behalf of that person or group is even more impactful and rewarding.

Taking on extra projects (especially cross-departmental), new areas you don't have expertise in, and board roles (inside/outside of the company) are great growth and expansion challenges. They are also rewarding if a job becomes boring or someone lacks motivation in their current role. We can become so fixed on only being "allowed" to do those tasks, we limit our opportunities to look for new areas to contribute and learn. I've also found advice on skill-building to be helpful to folks, including shadowing someone in an area of your company who has a specific skill like financial acumen or analysis. Learning from them will increase your marketability and ability to confidently take on new projects or assignments. This approach is anything but complacent.

Make the Shift

Here are some ways that individuals can overcome complacency and achieve their goals:

1. Work consistently at achieving your goals. Break down actions into a doable and measurable plan.

2. Find purpose and meaning in your goals. Determine what in your goals brings you fulfillment and excitement. This will help motivate you to achieve them.

3. Identify the value of what you CAN do brings to your team, company, and customers. Regarding what you can influence and the impact of the vision and strategy of the company: does this line up with your job description? Challenge it. You can do more, effectively.

4. Increase personal standards (pick one thing more you can do in your day). Think about "must" over "should." Raising your standards is a secret to life. If you do a good job nowadays you get poor rewards. Increasing standards increases rewards. Tony Robbins says, "People's lives are a direct reflection of the expectations of their peer group."

5. Put a due date on it. Create a sense of urgency around achieving goals.

Make the Shift

Here are some ways that managers and leaders can reduce compliance and complacency and increase integrity and commitment:

1. Allow others to have influence. Really let go and empower and enable your teams. They have great ideas and different views of how to achieve a goal or provide a service. Let them shine.

2. Challenge the status quo—in front of your teams. Encourage AND support a culture of continuous improvement and innovation. This also means supporting peer groups in front of your teams and behind closed doors if there is a culture of finger-pointing or lack of trust across teams.

3. Encourage experimentation. This allows for a natural flow from fear of failure. Allowing focus, time, and investment will bring back rewards in ways not expected. That includes commitment, contribution, and loyalty from your teams.

You can see how both compliance and complacency can hinder being our authentic selves in the workplace. There is a lot of shift happening in both of these areas as we are wanting more fulfillment in our jobs/careers and opportunities to learn.

Complexity Is a Killer

One of Tony Robbins' most famous quotes, "Complexity is the enemy of execution," has so much meaning inside and around it. There are so many ways we can look at complexity in the workplace and "why" we create it. So much of it ends up coming from an inauthentic place in an effort to prove ourselves, our value, our intelligence, and our qualifications. Overuse of complex industry terms, business slang, and phrases to explain business becomes ingrained in culture and an assumed expectation that everyone needs to speak and do in a complex way. What we should pursue is evolving our minds to a simplicity-first mindset. Understanding our audience, processes with minimal steps and fewer hand-offs, clear guidance in communications, and simple explanations of offerings are key. As our world evolves, everyone is looking for the "simple" in everything.

In simple terms, Robbins is suggesting that anything other than keeping things simple is a waste of your time and effort. Flipping his quote around for a second, there's a perspective that complexity is, in fact, the enemy of success. The problem with complexity is that it takes focus from a more simple and effective line of thought. In so doing, it clearly impacts confidence and understanding of what could be the message. This causes confusion and kills motivation.

When teams do not understand what is being asked, it causes frustration and missed goals. It's important to keep the message in simple terms (yet not dumbed down) so the audience, whether colleagues or customers, confidently understand your message. One of the biggest motivations to meeting team goals is being able to comprehend them. Overly technical terms shut people down. Processes to get anything done that are too complex do not create a good experience for either colleagues or customers/partners. Complex offerings dilute the value of what a company or team are trying to put out there. Teams struggle to align what they do each day with the value the company is trying to portray.

There are many companies going through transformation. Unfortunately, in an effort to simplify, they are actually making things more complicated. As Tony Robbins puts it, "Change is never a matter of ability. It's always a matter of motivation." If things are complex, it's not motivating to colleagues. When change shoves people deeper into a box, it's not motivating and won't be successful. If the change is not inclusive, it will also create an inauthentic alignment for colleagues, leading to disengagement.

At an individual level, complexity in our day can make us feel more valuable, but it doesn't provide fulfillment. Attaching complexity to value in an effort to feel that we are unique or needed is not a healthy way to work. It can ultimately backfire and take us into overwhelm. Letting go of this attachment can allow for more truly valuable activities and creation in our day. Allowing for our true first instinct to challenge existing processes or tasks we are doing (or are a part of within the company system process) will start challenging how we spend our day and allow us to shift to more purposeful contributions.

"Complexity is your enemy. Any fool can make something complicated. It is hard to make something simple," said serial entrepreneur, Richard Branson. I love this quote, as it totally calls out the overdoing it approach many put on making things complex just to prove something/themselves. The real talent and gift is to create it in a simple way. Whether it's a product, solution, process, or communication of value. Here is a complex mission statement of MoMA that could be so much simpler. "To collect, preserve, study, exhibit, and stimulate appreciation for and advance knowledge of works of art that collectively represent the broadest spectrum of human achievement at the highest level of quality, all in the service of the public and in accordance with the highest professional standards." How are customers/clients/donors and employees supposed to feel connected to that? Too complex and too long.

Unfortunately, with global business and technology expanding, there seems to be even more complexity setting in. Is it really necessary? There will be some complexity that lingers and it will be a matter of how to adaptively lead and work through it. Keeping things simple is actually quite easy. Our actions and the quality of our solutions can be affected by complexity and given that humans have a natural tendency to overcomplicate things, the status quo doesn't look like it will change unless we shift our approach to starting simple and shift our mindset around a need for complexity, essentially by being inventive, bold, and aggressive.

The key is to not put barriers to success up before you start. Taking a "simplicity first" way of working forward is almost certainly the way to remove most traces of complexity from getting deals done. Constantly look out for simple solutions to everything that you do, and where possible, develop that simplicity first mindset. Keep the box at bay and go for what will help customers and colleagues feel more connected and have a simple experience.

Make the Shift

Let go of ego and complexity mindset and look for the simple in our day. This can be used in how you decide to focus on tasks and projects as well.

1. Shift to big-picture thinking. So much complexity is in the parts. In a world of big picture, we can look for opportunities to simplify across departments, teams, programs, and products.

2. Give up the illusion of control. Let go of "knowing how everything works" and start from a place of not knowing and curiosity, allowing for creative solutions.

3. Let go of firefighting or reactive mindset as a strategy. This is so prevalent in the workplace and leads to using this strategy to align our values. Instead, proactively simplify and fix processes and problem areas so energy can be spent more wisely.

13

ULTIMATE CONTROL

Things don't spiral out of control when we surrender them; they spiral out of control when we try to control them!
——Marianne Williamson

Control and Attachment to Outcomes

This chapter will get into some of the "preferences" we habituate in the workplace, typically based on fear, not authenticity. Control and attachment to outcomes is one of my biggest "bad habits" that I have been working on. Compliance and complacency are some habits that we can fall into based on "not wanting to rock the boat." Complexity is a habit we accentuate to keep value attached to our identity and to showcase our intelligence. In reality, none of these habits are actually helpful, productive, effective, or healthy for us or our relationships in the workplace. Let's dive into control and attachment to outcomes first.

The definition of control according to *Merriam-Webster Dictionary* is "to have power over: Rule." This could be situations, people, or results. It is understandable to want to be in control of your life, and there is a healthy level of control we all must retain in order to direct our lives and pursue our goals and passions. However, if you have reached a point where you are wondering, "Am I controlling?" it's likely you've passed the point of healthy control. In reality, the only things we can control are our mind, state, and energy. Let's dive a bit into what's behind this need to control.

A need to control is rooted in the Six Human Needs, according to Tony Robbins.[9] *Certainty,* or the need to avoid pain, find comfort, and gain pleasure is one of the most basic human needs that causes control (survival mechanism). *Significance,* or the need to feel needed, unique, and special is the next most common human need that causes control. One of the paradoxes to significance is the need for *connection* (also a need of personality like certainty and significance). One of the great opportunities to make connection is in the workplace, in authentic ways fulfilling friendships are formed, and in controlling ways they are not. When control is attempted to be placed on people, whether to get them to do what you want, to be a "team," or to connect, it's under false pretenses and fails.

We think, "If I can control my circumstances in my job, all areas of my life will run smoothly." This can bleed over to managers controlling "how" their teams get work done to avoid failure or missing deadlines. This micromanagement is not healthy, nor does it allow for innovation and creativity from the team. The manager's control caps the potential of the team and business. We will touch on the remaining of these human needs in other sections.

The fear of failure and self-doubt really sparks much of the need to control, and when we feel threatened (not hitting goals, not meeting deadlines, feeling anxious), it feels like the only alternative is to pull out our control stick. I've also felt this need when overwhelm was setting in. The more out of control I felt (situations, results, people, activities, deadlines), the more overwhelm set in. My solution to that? Control it.

---

[9] Tony Robbins (Team Tony), "Why You Are The Way You Are, The 6 Factors That Are Behind Every Emotion And Behavior" *Tony Robbins,* https://www.tonyrobbins.com/mind-meaning/why-you-are-the-way-you-are/

Tony Robbins says, "Certainty is created within YOU, not by your environment."

Another behavior that tends to go with control is attachment to outcomes. Not only does this bring in a component of controlling, but also limits the types of solutions that can come in for outcomes because we can become so attached to "how" it happens. Why do we attach to outcomes? Fear of losing or not achieving something is probably the biggest reason. Excitement at achieving a goal, or feeling good about our contribution—the attachment to a result takes hold when you believe that in order to be happy, you "must have it," or you "should reach a goal." This attachment also arises from the anxious anticipation of a strong negative feeling if you do not reach your goal.

Are you too attached to outcomes? The ability to let go of your attachment to the outcome is so important to your success with any personal or professional goal. You can still be focused on your *intention* and be ready to take the necessary actions, while at the same time *letting go* of your attachment. Once we release our attachment to an outcome, it doesn't mean that we're any less interested in manifesting the goal. It simply means that we're less interested in the fear of not achieving it. We've shifted our attention away from fear because we feel safe. Having no expectations of actions and lowering your expectations of people is liberating and can lead you to a happier life, not to mention better relationships.

How do you know if you are too attached to outcomes?

1. Always feeling the need to know "how." The need to know how to do something before even getting started limits the experimentation and exploration of learning an even better way to do things.

2. Needing something now creates an attachment to timing. This is a big one and can actually end up becoming a barrier to the outcome unfolding.

3. Allowing others' judgments to influence your approach and decisions is an attachment that limits your own ability to learn, grow, and showcase your gifts.

4. Needing to control what someone else does (or doesn't do) can actually create resistance that prevents things from changing.

5. Fearing failure, that past experiences will repeat, or disappointing others can also create control and attachment to the outcome of a situation. In reality, most fear is created, it's not real, and we have the opportunity to challenge it.

In terms of pursuing goals, freeing yourself from attachments to a particular outcome has to do with comprehending that there are certain things you cannot control. *The Buddha once said that attachment is the cause of all suffering.* Deepak Chopra says the following about the Law of Detachment: 1) it allows yourself and others freedom to be who they are, 2) by not forcing solutions you allow solutions to spontaneously emerge, 3) uncertainty is essential and also your path to freedom.

Let's talk about another of the Six Human Needs: *uncertainty or variety*. It's amazing how personal growth leads you to wanting to shift from certainty to uncertainty/variety as it offers a more fulfilling and purpose-filled life with exciting unknown opportunities. When we release fear of uncertainty and the need to know everything that will happen in life, we create this freedom.

Practice letting go of what you cannot control or change. Nonattachment is freedom from things and situations. It is a realization of the truth of reality—that you and consciousness cannot be affected by anything. It is only the egoic mind that makes you believe otherwise. In the workplace, reducing your need to control situations, others, and outcomes can reduce how much energy you spend to get even better results. Trust your teams and each other to reduce the need to control and help each other overcome fear of failure through experimentation and creative solutions.

Make the Shift

Ten ways to detach from controlling outcomes and others and keep things simple:

1. Avoid giving advice unless asked.
2. Realize that you don't need to have all the answers (or know it all).
3. Focus on self, not what "should be done."
4. Let them experience their own choices.
5. Stop focusing on their behavior.
6. Allow for creative solutions to emerge (don't control the how).
7. Stop harping on them about their responsibilities.
8. Help only when asked.
9. Appreciate and compliment what they ARE doing well.
10. Let yourself off the hook, it's not your problem!

On Perfectionism

I feel that perfectionism fits nicely under the topic of ultimate control. Perfectionism can be fear-based and typically rides alongside of both expectations of self and others and attachment to outcomes. This has been one of my challenges over time, and much of it has been based on societal expectations and conditioning, generational conditioning, and fear of failure. I'd like to share how this was such an underlying issue for me over most of my adult life. Being a perfect mother, wife, daughter, or employee is not healthy. When you try to fit a role or identity that is structured with unrealistic expectations, you can lose your authenticity. I've found that I also get into a cycle of just doing instead of being.

First, it's interesting to look at the definition of perfectionism. The best definition I'd like to share is from Brené Brown. She says, "Perfectionism is the belief that if we do things perfectly and look perfect, we can minimize or avoid the pain of blame, judgment, and shame. Perfectionism is a twenty-ton shield that we lug around, thinking it will protect us, when in fact it's the thing that's really preventing us from being seen."[10] This is so true and digs a bit deeper into the impact on trying to earn approval and putting achievement and performance above our actual worth. It ends up becoming a mask in and of itself, keeping us protected and "shielded" from failure, disappointment, and rejection. Brené Brown says, "When perfectionism is driving us, shame is riding shotgun and fear is that annoying backseat driver"

When I think back to "why" perfectionism was such an issue for me, there are a few key reasons: my need for control of outcomes or end states, pressure to have it all together, and fear of disappointing, looking bad, and others failing (colleagues, children, etc.). Unfortunately, every single one of these situations really happened, which is why it was added to the drive for perfection over the years. Is it good to be thorough and accurate? Of course! What isn't helpful though, is the impact perfectionism has on authenticity. When you are trying to control every single thing in life and be the most organized, you lose some of the important pieces of your true self. You can lose vulnerability, truth, trust (in self and others), delegation, and empowerment. You also lose a ton of time that you could be spending on self, family, or hobbies. The extra effort that goes into being perfect is exhausting.

I know I'm not the only one who struggles with perfectionism. Typically, some of the limiting beliefs and limitations of our mind create stories of disappointment or failure. Living in the past and/or future creates most of the pressure to drive perfection. Our mind starts going and before you know it, one thought becomes some big story of a major issue that will happen if you don't get the dang grocery list done. So, is being organized a bad thing? Of course not! Expecting yourself to be perfect at it is. I remember having spreadsheets of all of my boy's baseball schedules (park ball, all stars, travel league). It was a massive color-coded spreadsheet

---

[10] Brené Brown, "The Gifts of Imperfection: Let Go of Who You Think You're Supposed to Be and Embrace Who You Are", *Hazelden Publishing*, August 27, 2010

that, yes, was very helpful to stay organized, but a lot of work to create that was probably not necessary. I've started challenging myself on many activities that I thought were necessary to keep it together that instead are probably not necessary. Guess what? Life seems to work out the same or even better!

Perfectionism outside of work can impact work or even a sense of self in one or the other environments. Let's say you are struggling in the home environment. You missed a kid's doctor appointment, submitted a bill late, or forgot a necessary ingredient for a meal. The extra pressure this puts on being perfect in the workplace goes up. The need to feel like you've got at least one area on target is a pull that does not let go unless you recognize it. If you get sucked in, it becomes a shield and sword game of perfection. An all-in attitude (and energy), proving self, and taking on more than you can handle become the sword fight and then you protect with the shield through needing approval, achievement, and acknowledgment. This goes both ways. Struggles at work push the need for perfectionism at home. It's sometimes the point of overwhelm when we finally release control and surrender a bit. Once we do this it tends to reset everything, until we fall back into our perfectionism behavior again.

I've learned to trust others, the process, and to take the action I need to, but let it go after that. Forcing things to happen is not the best option and it's exhausting and frustrating. Letting go of control on how others are navigating life is also important. I found this challenge mostly with my kids. I never want to see them fail, so I try to be their lighthouse, giving them guidance and looking ahead for the potential issues because I already went through them. This doesn't necessarily help them the majority of the time, because they can't build their own intuitive and attentive muscle to anticipate what could happen next. My holding a strong grip on their every action, to-do, and anticipated outcome was frustrating them and exhausting me. Once I started to trust them to make their own choices and show them love and support along the way, everything got easier for all of us.

My favorite mantra is "everything is going to be OK." Yes, this has literally calmed me down over and over when things got overwhelming or stressful (or unknown). I take a deep breath and say my mantra. Try it, it really helps! What I've found is that whatever it is typically ends up being alright!

Make the Shift

Follow these steps and answer the questions to loosen your grip:

1. Pick three things in your life (work/home) you want to loosen up on.
2. Determine why you feel you have to control that activity or task.
3. Review each of the outcomes you expect. How do you typically try to control the outcome, and what is the actual outcome?
4. Decide if there is an opportunity to reduce your grip and let it flow. How does that make you feel?
5. Delegate or outsource the tasks you can hand off to others.
6. Repeat with three more and keep going.

14

LET'S GET REAL WITH WHAT WE ARE DOING

It's not the daily increase, but the daily decrease. Hack away at the unessential.
——Bruce Lee

Busy and Grit

Chances are you're losing your sense of self and not even aware of it. "Workism" makes us believe that we are what we do for our job or pay-related work, which leads us to adapt a work-obsessed mindset. When we see our peers, colleagues, or idols promoting their early-morning workouts, their late nights in the office, their after-work work, we start to believe that *everybody's hustling*. But often we see what others want us to see, and it makes us believe that we're not doing enough.

Grit has become a badge of honor, and while I do believe in grit, I think it has been taken a little too far. It becomes very difficult to positively use grit to keep going continuously without burnout setting in. "Too much of anything is not good for you." This is a phrase we use in our house a lot. It helps us to keep a check on not going overboard on anything. That includes how much energy and time we put into anything. I've learned that not everything needs to be a full-out focus and energy push to get it done and by a certain time. Finding flow is my new grit, and it's such a better place to be.

Here's how I used to do things. Work, work, work. I was thinking about work on my commute and at home, working all day fully (even late), and then sometimes I would come home and continue working, depending on the special assignment or extra project going on and whether the kids had activities. Grit was how I got through it. Push, push, push. The more I took on, the more I depended on my grit to get it done. This can be a slippery slope, since what I found is that it got to the point where I was always looking for the vacation or "light at the end of the tunnel" in order to "just get through this thing." Starting out excited about a project or opportunity to learn something new brings in a certain energy. In my case, as soon as one special assignment would end, another would begin, and this became eight years of back-to-back special assignments and projects on top of my day-job responsibilities. Grit became my enemy and unhappiness. Of course, I allowed it!

Another of these limits used in the workplace as a value badge is "being busy." Busy, busy, busy. "Busy" has been replaced with "too busy," "far too busy," or "absolutely buried." It's true that being productive often means being busy, but it's only true up to a point. This can be such a cover for what we really can be focused on, and the fact we are probably overcommitted. Being busy makes us look like we are working hard; we feel good about our day and that we're adding value. It's more for us than what is actually needed to progress the business. When it comes down to it, more than half of what we do in a day, including way too many useless or unproductive meetings, makes us look busy, but is not really effectively adding value to our customers or business. Busy bleeds into personal life as well—busy with kids (running them to practices for this and that), house chores, and other tasks that keep us hopping. At some point busy turns into overwhelm.

Just because our calendar is full and we have three presentations to create today does not mean the outcome of those things is going to actually impact the value we provide in our job. Take a step back to really look at "why" we are so busy and start challenging not only ourselves, but those around us as to why there are so many meetings, or why there are so many presentations where decisions are not made, or why there are so many people involved.

I really like Greg McKeown's approach in his book *Essentialism: The Disciplined Pursuit of Less* and have adopted parts his method. Essential intent is the concrete inspiration where one decision made can eliminate one thousand future decisions. Make decisions versus wordsmithing (love this one), say "no" gracefully (requires trading popularity for respect), uncommit when needed (without guilt/attachment), and get over the fear of missing out (you don't need to attend every meeting, just share your thoughts and trust others to make decisions). How do we make choices and trade-offs, and narrow things to the vital few from the "trivial many," and create ease in doing the "vital few" things?

There are many ways to break away from being busy to being intentional in how we spend our time and creativity and use our knowledge and wisdom to create progress. This includes:

- Slowing down to really assess how we are spending our time.
- Working to eliminate the belief that we have to be busy to compete or justify our value.
- Learning how to say "no" and stay focused.
- Reducing how many times you check your phone.
- Blocking time in your calendar.
- Scheduling time to get tasks done read work email, and set meetings.
- Improving how you organize your day and prioritize your tasks.

- Tracking and budgeting your time to determine how you are actually spending it in your day.
- Identifying intentions (clear and essential), value of tasks/meetings (what's the benefit), and the cost of what you are doing (what you invest and give up for each).
- Reducing commitments—don't overcommit or overdeliver
- Giving yourself more time to get your work done.
- Using tools to prioritize and set real intentions to really dive into what is truly necessary and what we truly need to be doing in a day.

Getting a reality check on grit and busy ways of pushing through your day will help to get to a flow and feeling more purposeful in your day.

Make the Shift

Seven signs you are too busy:

1. You can't remember the last time you took a day off.
2. Eating any of your meals is done in tandem with other tasks.
3. You are consistently more tired when you get up in the morning than when you go to bed.
4. Close friends and family have stopped asking for your time.
5. You dread getting up in the morning.
6. The most exercise you get is sprinting from one commitment to the next.
7. "Survival mode" is your only mode.

Rounding Out Part 1

It's hard to see all of the things showing up in our day, team, and life because we are so close to it. We are wired to adapt and survive so we adapt to the environment we are in regardless of whether we truly believe in it, accept it, or want it. The limitations we can deal with on a daily basis that impact who we are, who we show up as, and who we want to be creates conflict with our true selves. The key areas of focus that allow us to change what showing up to work means to us are:

- Reducing distractions that create overwhelm and lead to escapism.
- Connecting to our energy and learning to better manage it to reduce burnout.
- Setting clear expectations and reducing judgment.
- Seeking truth in our mindset and reducing the negative self-talk.
- Telling our story instead of having it formulated in a box.
- Seeking realistic goals and timelines without controlling every outcome.
- Speaking up instead of being compliant and reducing complexity in our day.
- Balancing busy and grit with being productive.
- Being in cause versus effect.
- Setting healthy boundaries.

In order to reduce stress that has increasingly become 24–7 and improve our self-worth, self-care and fulfillment in life—especially our work life—we need to focus on the shifts we need to make and support those around us as they make theirs. The opportunity to make shifts inside-out to free ourselves from old conditioning, being "boxed" up, and masking our true selves enables us to use our subconscious as our superpower. Supporting these shifts to take place in ourselves and coworkers starts to shift the environment and culture we work in. Encouraging and fully embracing our authenticity allows for the rest of our gifts to emerge. This is the exciting outcome of doing the work.

In part 2 I'll dive into some of the most valuable of these elevated gifts, the characteristics that shine through, and how these gifts are evolving not only business and culture, but us as a human race. Encouraging these gifts instead of undervaluing or fearing people bringing these gifts forward in their day-to-day is how we will truly revolutionize authenticity in the workplace.

PART TWO
YOUR AUTHENTIC
ELEVATED GIFTS

15

LIVING IN PASSIONATE BELIEF

The best way to predict the future is to create it.
——Abraham Lincoln

Évocateur

Now more than ever, those special gifts need to shine! Bring them out of hiding, out of the closet, and share them with the world. So many protect these next two gifts out of fear of not being accepted, or being viewed as "out there," a dreamer, or "too much" in the business world. Yet these are the gifts that help us transition into the future by helping others to see the vision of the future as well. The gift of being an Évocateur encourages an inspired flow of creativity, creative ideas, solutions, approaches, and ways of doing the work.

You are the Évocateur of embodiment by evoking collaborative leadership through your creativity, fluidity, magic, presence, and inclusive perspective.

You have an energy that is electrifying and positive. Others are drawn to you for how bright you shine, especially when you are flowing in creativity. This might be in solution design, innovation, marketing, training, organizational design, or a vision for a better way. You challenge status quo without it looking like you are. You are a muse, confident in creative expression and the ability to create. Your openness to change and novel ideas comes with ease. You love to play with ideas and new ways of doing things. You thrive on encouraging an environment of playfulness, humor, spontaneity, and unpredictability. You inspire others to unleash their creativity!

I've worked with quite a few Évocateurs over the years. Many were called dreamers in the business world because they always had great ideas, but could never quite bring them to fruition. Yet I look back at some of their ideas and guess what? About five years later someone brought them to fruition. It's like that invention you came up with a few years ago and didn't act on, and then—poof—there it is on TV invented by someone else. Others were taken seriously, but not given the resources or support to bring the ideas into being. Then, of course, they became part of the bag of "that didn't work in the past."

I love Elizabeth Gilbert's theory on "ideas" in her book *Big Magic*. I have seen so many proof points of this as well. The theory is that ideas are sent to us (probably by our muses—check out *The War of Art* by Steven Pressfield as well), and we will only have so much time to take action on them before they are then sent to someone else. The idea may be granted back to you when you are ready, but many times it is accepted and actioned by someone else. Then it's on to the next idea and the cycle continues. I think about writing this book. I've had a hundred topics I wanted to write on over the years. Every year it changed with where I was in life, what I was passionate about at that time, and what I felt was important to me. Yet I didn't take action to write on any of those ideas. This one I did.

The impact Évocateurs have is the ability to keep things real, fun, and simple. They don't overcomplicate something to "give it value." They give it value by the passion they fuel their creative ideas with. They bring excitement to rally others, which gets others to not only buy in, but integrate and embody the ideas. They share and bring others in to create an inclusive perspective. They are not stubborn about their idea, and they love feedback to build on the idea. It's so important that the Évocateur is heard, supported, and given not only the space, but resources to bring ideas to light.

The Évocateur struggles with NOT being able to share their gift in the business world because of time constraints/pressing deliverables causing procrastination. Also, you may feel scattered, feel too serious (due to old expectations), or have a hard time expressing yourself. Fear of being judged for being silly or for "playing," and fear of being left out impact the creative flow. I've seen many folks come up with super-creative ideas and not be able to articulate an "execution" plan (a requirement in the business world).

Why not partner with someone who has that gift? A perfect example of this is my partnership with Pat Gehant as we cofounded the Exploratory Lab Boot Camp. While this is a community engagement, it brings together both the education and business worlds. She is the Évocateur—creative, partnering, collaborative, and "the dreamer"—while I am the executor. She is inclusive with all levels of education and then with business. She sees how the vision can unfold, and she is a great storyteller (another gift we'll cover later). Pat inspires me to see her vision and has kept it evolving over the past eight years. I then devise a plan to bring it to reality, including how it can flow, resources to bring it to reality, and keeping it practical enough to get results and scale.

We both joke about how great our synergies work together and how we couldn't deliver the "big" idea without each other. All it may take is partnering up to fully leverage your Évocateur gift in the business world. Listen to the Évocateur. Their "dreams" typically come true, and whether you are that person or have the ability to support them, acknowledge this is a gift.

Edgewalker

The Edgewalker is one of my favorites, gifting everyone through inclusiveness (giving a voice to all) like a megaphone. They have a magical ability to create a safe space to share ideas and issues. They are great at showing all members they are valued for their contributions, and giving safe space for them to share their concerns, ideas, and how they would like to participate or what they see is needed. They put themselves out there without it feeling like they are, because they are so passionate about what they see, hear, and feel. The Edgewalker invests in others through one-on-one conversations to share their vision and spend time helping others to connect to it. They have instinctual integrity and are highly intuitive (trusting the unknown through instincts and inner knowing). Many entrepreneurs have the Edgewalker gift.

As an Edgewalker, you bring the collective together in the big picture and are a grounded catalyst through challenge.

As an Edgewalker, you are a big-picture visionary, passionate, and untamed in bringing your ideas to the masses. You magnetize teams and community with wisdom and integrity and are a go-to for both personal and professional guidance. You are a cutting-edge creatrix bringing forth bold ideas and challenging status quo and outmoded systems. I like to visualize the Edgewalker as having one foot in the here and now and one foot in the future. They literally walk the edge of the earth. One foot can slip into the unknown while the other stays planted. They act as a bridge between these worlds to help those who struggle to see the big picture and future do so without it being so far out there. They are grounded in understanding the practical of the here and now.

You are a powerhouse: bold and unapologetic, and you can be shocking and catalyzing. You are vibrant, almost wild, even weird (yay), and stretch us beyond our existence, beyond what we know. Your collaborative leadership is one of the power tools for shifting old norms and creating a visionary path others can get behind. You find beauty in dismantling, knowing creation will be more impactful. You are a recordkeeper of the most trans-formative moments of your team members, company (community, family, person) by bringing authenticity and vulnerability (nakedness) to the table through connecting the dots. You are also a great bullshit detector!

You don't have to feel it to see it, and you don't have to see it to feel it. The Edgewalker is comfortable with extremes including disruptive change and contentment. They smoothly navigate challenging things in life, working through them with flow and ease (even the difficult ones). Basically, they are pretty grounded and steady in stressful, chaotic, and challenging times. They are comfortable with the uncomfortable. This helps to calm others around them. They filter out the noise and chaos to reduce the sting of situations and change, allowing others to smoothly transition as well. This gift is very useful in creating bold new ideas and solutions in an inclusive and collaborative way. It's also a necessary gift in companies going through transformation or creation. Natural leadership qualities of an Edgewalker include holding space when everything else is falling apart. The Edgewalker navigates transition and change with ease and helps others do so as well.

Some of the challenges the Edgewalker can experience are separation (from self and others) and a feeling of limitation and lack caused by feeling the resources you need to accomplish an idea, vision, job, cause, or people-focused effort, won't be available to you. The feeling of pushing against the edges and never quite feeling like you are where you want to be is a real frustration. Feeling separated can cause competition, comparison, and expert status (either in the more extreme or less for each). This may cause an Edgewalker to feel like they can be too much, too intense, and not valued. It can also be a lonely world. Newly-bloomed Edgewalkers struggle to understand why others "just don't get it" and can feel rejected or lost. I've seen this quite a few times. Once they realize it's not them, it's the others who just aren't quite ready (or not the right group) for what they are bringing to light, it shifts their approach and patience.

In old systems, the Edgewalker can feel trapped or caged with no space to self-express and can have a powerful yearning to feel free and rebel against rules or authority (which then creates conflict because it looks like disrespect). How many times have we felt this way in the business world (the words politics and bureaucracy come to mind)? Let's not forget rebelliousness is also a gift!

I have seen some great Edgewalkers overcome the challenges through not attaching to expectations and letting go of a project or change once it's complete. It's done, let it go. Focus on connecting through collaboration and inclusion to help fight separation. Ask others how they have been able to get resources (maybe it's a phased approach and not in the order you may think it should be). When you feel like you've "crossed the line" (I'm sorry I have to laugh when I write this because what the hell line, who created it and when was it created?) and are being "too much" or "too bold" with your ideas, statements, etc., don't recede. Ask questions versus telling to truly get others to open up their thinking in a way they are able to process.

16

EMBRACING AUTHENTIC LEADERSHIP

Integrity is a vulnerability that disguises nothing.
——Ariel Spilsbury

Servant Leader

Servant leadership is the "new" way of leading. Servant leadership in its truest form is an act of devotion. It is not about giving or getting, it is a circuitry of love ever flowing without conditions. So how does this translate into the business environment and its leaders? How many folks have worked for someone who truly felt that person was devoted to your personal/professional needs? Maybe a few ... or less? The patriarchal system has created a hierarchy, behaviors, and of course, expectations over millennium that created a system of the leader/subordinate relationship and expectations. How does that all of a sudden shift in the practice of servant leadership where leaders truly "care" about the needs of their, well, subordinates?

The way we will slowly and truly shift this paradigm is through those who are on a mission to use their gifts by being Servant Leaders. I call this a gift because, honestly, there is a lot that needs to change in the business environment and community at large before being a Servant Leader is actually authentic, received, and expected. Today there is a lot of mistrust in work cultures. Even the attempt to "be a Servant Leader" without authenticity is a disaster waiting to happen. If you don't fully feel from your heart care or at least empathy for your team members, then you can't be a Servant Leader. Right?

This gift is not always easy for those who truly are Servant Leaders. They are consistent with their words, intentions, and actions. They listen (hard for all of us!) and they are compassionate (this still has a long way to go to be accepted in the business world) to the needs of their colleagues and community members. They strive for excellence and try to learn as much as possible to be the most supportive of their colleagues, company, and community. They don't bullshit! They admit when they don't know something versus spewing anecdotal or incorrect/unvalidated information. They don't lay down judgments of others who don't follow their same thinking. They don't have personal agendas and don't manipulate situations or people. Are you starting to see why I make the statement servant leadership is rare? We see this every day.

You are a Servant Leader because you authentically value those around you and your actions meet the expectations of integrity you speak of.

You are a Servant Leader because you listen to the needs of others. You don't wait for the ball to drop before taking action, and you ask instead of waiting to be told what is going on with your teams. You foresee roadblocks and potential barriers and start working on removing them even before you ask your team to charge full steam ahead. You are the one who speaks up when it's not popular to do so. You ask the questions that are meaningful and important and not because you want to showcase your expertise. You speak on behalf of the team's needs and ensure their voice is heard. You trust and are trusted. You make decisions with ease and without glory, ego, or expectation of acknowledgment. You'll be the first to admit you don't know something and give your team member who is the expert the floor. You motivate your team to own results and outcomes through showing them the value they bring. You filter the crazy and chaos to keep your team focused and committed. You're always learning. You'll do the battles behind the scenes and not talk about it to others. You are who we need in business and in the world.

Back to my comment about not being authentic: one of the challenges of servant leadership is when there is a push to "become" Servant Leaders, yet it's done in an inauthentic way. If there wasn't empathy toward others previously, it's kind of hard to make that magically appear. Connection, trust, and openness happens when there are two people who create this for each other. Doing good for others (take an action, offer to help, make a donation) because you want to be a Servant Leader yet your heart isn't into it can negate the energy of exchange. It neutralizes the "good." Be the leader who embodies nonjudgment and acts as a holder of presence, warmth, and support by creating space for others.

Seeker

It's a reality that business leaders in "some" companies have severely struggled with integrity over recent years. Just Google the headlines. Our species needs to demand a change in integrity, and each one of us brings that to the table. The gift of integrity is one that is visible and predictable. It's what we can trust. It's always improving.

You are a Seeker because your gift of integrity brings predictability, trust, and a safe space to those you engage.

In the simplest terms, integrity is a governance of your values. Your gift of integrity sings in the hearts of those you engage, transact, or collaborate with. Why? Because they trust you, you reduce stress for them, and bring the predictability of fairness and openness. You are deeply true to yourself. Your ability to be ambitious and autonomous gives you vision to expanded possibilities. The Seeker is all about seeking truth and not conformity. Think about how you have been in situations with those who have integrity and those who do not. You FEEL it.

I've found when I'm working with people in business or the community and my values don't align with those folks or organizations, I immediately feel it in my body. My chest and throat tighten up and my heart races. It's my built-in radar that this is NOT where I want to be. I've learned NOT to just deal with it or them (if a person). I try to disengage, decline engagement, or simply ignore/avoid. I know the last one is wimpy, but it has worked. For me this includes vendors, customers (nobody should be off the hook!), neighbors, or even organizations in the community. I've had all of these situations, as I'm sure most of you have as well.

In reality, not everyone you work or live with has the same values or integrity you do. Now, if it's a significant problem across the organization or group, then YES, get out! The most important thing to note is that in the challenge of staying engaged, you can become easily trapped by ego identity, yet resent the company and/or people because it's not what your heart believes or wants you to do. It will eat away at your soul.

Integrity is something many talk about, but what can be challenging is when you try to live by integrity in a space where others don't want you to. This may include certain decisions you are being asked to make or in treating others (exclusion). It's up to you to determine the trade-off (mostly for your own conscience). In a controlling, authoritative culture, this could actually be an issue. If individuals cannot work according to their own integrity and are being asked to do things they don't believe in, it can cost them their job if they don't do it. The opportunity here is for leaders to do a double-check on their integrity and the culture they are influencing. Everyone can make the change to truly adopt their gift of integrity.

I really like *The 4 Agreements: A Practical Guide to Personal Freedom* written by Don Miguel Ruiz. They are self-explanatory and easy to remember, but maybe a couple are not so easy to practice.

1. Be impeccable with your word.
2. Don't take it personally.
3. Don't make assumptions.
4. Always do your best.

I tend to take things personally at times, and honestly, it puts me on a roller coaster of emotions, and most of the time unnecessarily. Instead of just letting it go and flow. I have tried over time to not make assumptions and even put extra effort into discovering truth so I have facts, not blame or assumptions. Interestingly though, I have found this to be even more important in being a parent than at work. No matter what, you do you, and don't feel pressured to act like someone else, play games, or manipulate others. Stick to your values and act with integrity.

17

CHANNELING GENIUS

I am not an originator but a transmitter.
——Confucius

Messenger

We aren't fixed systems ... we are receivers and transmitters. Humans are the most complex creature in the multiverse. Why? Because we have an ego self and an intuitive self. They rarely see eye to eye! The ego self has to know every answer, control your behavior and actions in the past and the future, and set goals for every little thing. Your intuitive self flows, and is present, compassionate, and creative. Allowing for that flow to be nourished opens up the ability to trust and receive intuitive messages. Sometimes you may just feel something is right and your Messenger comes out to represent the whole. Sometimes you bring into being (from who the hell knows where) solutions, ideas and visions, and the story to explain them just flows. I used to joke that on my way home from work, as soon as I hit the Bayside Bridge (about eight minutes from my parking spot), solutions would just come to me. I guess it was getting out of an environment of tasks, meetings, and distractions into freed-up space in order to receive those messages that did it, and it was super impactful. Heck yea, I listened!

As a Messenger you are a vessel to carry the message into reality on behalf of the whole.

Have you noticed there are certain people (maybe you) who others constantly confide in around issues, potential challenges/opportunities, or ideas? It's not because they are designated to be the Messenger. It's because those folks trust that person and KNOW their voice will be heard through them. The Messenger is the one who will step forward to share what needs to be shared. Even if it means being uncomfortable. They put the greater good above their own and leverage their intuition to guide them in "how" they deliver the message.

As a Messenger, you are the one who is in tune with the people, the focus, the priority, the strategy, and the need. You bring forward important feedback, guidance, and outcomes because you are a great listener to the energy of the organization. You ensure the message is inclusive and full. You step out of your own comfort zone for the greater good. You embrace and embody the messages you share, which creates an energetic connection to others. You are a relevant key to connection of the whole. Your intuition is your channel and your message is your gift.

Messengers don't have it easy though. Many times these are tough messages that need to be spoken. Sometimes fear comes to the forefront. I can't tell you how many times I've brought forward a message and then said, "Well, I'll probably be fired for sharing that." Nonetheless, I still believed in it and KNEW it needed to be brought forward. Regardless of whose ego it affected.

Messengers are not the bearers of bad news. Many messages they need to share are wake-up calls, opportunities to shift and stimulate evolution or revolution, and may bring peace and stability to those needing to hear the message. I love the analogy of death and rebirth. Of course, our soul may take this journey, but within life we actually have these acts happen all the time, not in a physical sense, but in a metaphoric sense,—in our lives, our jobs, our relationships, our companies, or our projects. At some point "birth" was given to spark it up and get it going, and potentially at some point "death" happened to tear it down (especially if it was no longer serving us). The point of "rebirth" is when new creation happens and, of course, we typically say, "Dang, this is so much better." I believe Messengers stimulate much of this cycle in the world, which is great!

One of the challenges of the Messenger gift is the need for validation versus just going for it. When they bring something forward and it's rejected, they feel rejected, and it's hard to then put themselves in that position again. The Messengers struggling with this can establish a board, community, or support team to run their messages past to get feedback or simple validation, if that is what they might need. There is a heavy burden a Messenger carries, but the good they bring to so many and to the organization or community is truly heroic.

Transmitter

I view the Transmitter gift as something that was "turned on." It's about being open to those messages, genius ideas, and solutions that just pop into your head or come out of your mouth. The gift is tuning in and turning it on. We all have it! We all have inner knowing, intuition, and inner wisdom. It's all how we open up to it, listen to it, and embrace it. The Transmitter trusts what comes through and shares it in a way that aligns with the message they are sharing. I love the book *The War of Art* by Steven Pressfield. His message is about reducing the resistance that we have, which holds back our creative genius. He brings muses (and others) into the picture as those sending the messages we are here to receive. Many times over the years when something would come out of my mouth that sounded fantastic, I'd say, "Oh, that was my muse." I had no idea where it came from. Freaking cool, huh? I've talked to many people over the years who feel the same way.

There are quite a few amazing Transmitters in my life. The one thing I've noticed about each of them is that when they are "channeling," they sniff or their nose gets itchy. I've just noticed this because I have access to them—they don't know each other. I wonder if it's the throat chakra and third eye chakra working together, and the nose is an antenna.

You are a Transmitter ... you are a Transmitter because you are a big picture thinker who channels genius.

As a Transmitter, you have a very specific view of insights that comes from deep intuition. You are a natural synthesizer of disparate ideas and systems, which in this day and age leads to transformation. One of my favorite methods of this gift is storytelling. A Transmitter is a visionary storyteller good at structuring stories, ideas, and visions. They are open to the ideas that want to make their way here and channel the genius into a big picture. They are open to solutions that come through, and they open their channel to bring in the information that inspires others. This may even be inspirational words or direction.

Many times the Transmitter brings in ideas or solutions too soon. Sometimes this can be frustrating for the Transmitter, as timing and audience either accept or brush off the vision the transmitter shares. I personally have felt this frustration in giving opinions of potential future outcomes we should watch out for or expanding the vision of the big picture, only to have folks blow off the ideas in an effort to keep things more near-term or if they view them as unimportant. Guess what? Yep, those future indicators typically came to fruition. Sigh!

Sometimes ideas are just too early to feel "real," and sometimes the audience you share visionary ideas with is just not the right audience! I mentor a few men and women who struggle with being a Transmitter in a world where thinking is short-term: daily/monthly/quarterly and/or tactical. I share my story of experimentation in changing up the audience, or one-on-one campaigning, or better timing, or multiple repositioning. I end up telling them it's not worth being frustrated over. Not everyone receives information the same way or can shift it to big picture, fully entangled with multi-sequencing outcomes, and it's OK. It's not a reflection on you, and it doesn't mean the message is wrong.

The challenge part is not trying for the sake of "being right"! That ends up becoming the ego self versus your intuitive self, where the vision was born and loses intention. Also, the reason I try to address the frustration part of the Transmitter gift not being received is because it can cause us to reduce trust in our intuitive gift (remember that darn ego is ALWAYS trying to be in control). One of the ways I do a check on my intuition is by checking into my physical body when I make decisions, good and bad. I feel the ones that end up being good decisions in my heart space (pressure, expansion, excitement). I feel the ones that end up being not so good decisions in my sacral chakra (deep dullness in my lower belly).

Throughout history, Messengers and Transmitters have been crucial to evolution and revolution. Without them, we would still be in survival mode for part of our evolution as a species. Don't resist your intuition, those nudges you feel, hear, speak, or write. You are bringing vision forward.

18

BRINGING TO LIFE

The easiest thing is to react. The second easiest is to respond.
But the hardest thing is to initiate.
——Seth Godin in *Tribes*

Creator

I think there is such a loss of belief in our society. The belief in our gift of creating, being creative, bringing into existence something born in our minds and hearts. Everyone is born with the gift of creating. It does not take much to rip that sense of confidence of this gift right out of us (typically while we are young). Creativity, creating, and being a Creator all come from a sense of bringing vision to life. Unfortunately, when we think we are not creative (typically tied to art, performing arts, music, creative problem-solving, etc.), we lump all of those pieces of creating together and toss them out the door. You are a Creator because you generate: from a vision, feeling, thought, or emotion. Even as we may recover from old wounds and open up that Creator door, there are current adulting behaviors that will still hold it down, including not giving yourself space to create and not tapping into your resources.

Being a Creator does not only mean writing a book, whipping up some concoction in the kitchen that is to die for, or creating a piece of art. It means using your gift to bring to life something from within you. I've had so many thoughts that led to big ideas, that led to initiatives, that led to new business practices. I didn't realize how important it is to allow space for the initial idea or seed to get started. Seeds take time to germinate, sprout, and grow into something that maybe you didn't even fully imagine at the beginning. The point is that you got it started and tended to it! The most important part of shaping your idea is through storytelling in a way that others can align to. Being a visionary storyteller is a superpower for Creators.

You are a Creator through your ability to provide structure to vision to bring something into being.

You are a Creator because you take action on your vision. You use your imagination to find solutions. You are confident in your abilities to build. You see solutions/creations come into being. You know what it takes, are resourceful, and bring your ideas to life. You share your ideas with others without fear they will "steal" them. You are able to start with a blank canvas to create a plan, idea, solution, process, organization, marketing campaign, tool, software, policy, presentation, message, vision, strategy, mission, business model, engagement model, or basically anything else from scratch. This doesn't mean you can't bring others into the creation process; it just means you drive it.

One of the challenges of the Creator gift is not sharing ideas due to a fear of rejection. This may be due to experience, existing culture, or lack of confidence in the creation. Another can be not bringing it to fruition by not tapping into resources or not getting support to bring it to fruition. In a fast-paced world, everything is expected now. This may cause a Creator to rush through the process and not be happy with the results.

The most important piece of advice to get started or to keep your Creator gift going is you don't need to know all of the answers or how things will turn out (outcomes). Experiment and adjust along the way. The more space and time you provide your creation, the more it will evolve and grow. Being buried in tasks and execution mode holds you back. Give yourself space and time to tap into your gifts.

Generator

There are many gifts I've shared that proactively bring ideas to the table, but I'm going to share one that is all about waiting. To work in response instead of proactively. Waiting for their intuition to tell them to respond. The gift of executing on those items that truly need their help bringing them into reality and not being distracted by so many ideas and solutions, but instead waiting for the ones they take on and own.

Generators are the life force and energizers of the world. They are the doers, yet they aren't here to do everything. They immerse themselves in their own process. When they are engaged in what is correct for them, they create incredible results that benefit everything and everyone around them. They continue to build on their mastery over time. The glory and power of the Generator is in their ability to respond to life. Not to be chasing after things, but to wait to respond to life as it comes to them, to honor what their intuition responds to.

You are a Generator because you trust your intuition and use it to determine what it is you need to respond to and focus on.

You are a Generator because you trust your inner guidance on knowing what is correct for you. You use your own process to create and have the inner authority to focus on what aligns best. You have a strategy to how you work and constantly fine-tune your process. You trust your intuition and use it to determine what it is you need to respond to and focus on. You know how to get it done and others trust you to do so. You communicate updates and are not afraid to escalate when you hit barriers.

This gift is so underestimated in the workplace. I think there is this "new" expectation that everyone needs to bring all ideas forward, be strategic, and execute. Unfortunately, that isn't realistic. What is, however, is appreciating the Generator for what they make happen. They take the Creator's ideas and execute on them to bring them into reality. I've found this gift to be very helpful to ensure consistency and realization of an idea or solution. They may have some project management skills which give them structure and process.

One challenge of Generators is when they don't have realistic timelines to work from, it hinders their ability to get the job done. They may become frustrated and quit altogether. They need the time to work their own process. They may also be rash in making decisions, and mostly they need to take their time. Another challenge is getting stuck in expectations and focusing on something that is not correct for them. Giving yourself permission not to work on something that is not right for you and in the timeline you need is the best way to break out of this challenge. Old conditioning can hold you back from your full Generator gift.

19

INNOVATION IS THE OUTCOME

Creativity is thinking up new things. Innovation is doing new things.
——Theodore Levitt

Experimenter

Innovation has been a way we have moved forward in many areas of the world, how we live, and how we solve problems. This includes health care, technology, safety, education, and connectedness. One of the underlying gifts of an innovator is experimentation (with a lack of fear of failure). When you had to do a science experiment in school, there was a process to follow. Either the experiment proved your hypothesis or it didn't (or you found an alternative along the way). We have so many ideas that come into our minds, and many times we just ignore them because we aren't sure they will work or be valuable enough.

Experimentation is a true gift, as it goes against all of the conditioning we were raised with and especially pushes through that ole fear of failure we all seem to hold onto very tightly. I've found and have actually "experimented" with the use of the word, actions, and outcomes to help teams move forward without dwelling on failure. If it doesn't work, move on to the next! Ten ideas to start with will spark curiosity and passion, a hundred ideas typically brings forward success, and one thousand ideas

149

will bring forward innovation. The gift of experimenting is how new ideas become new programs, new offerings, new messaging, new products, new services, and new training. It's important that we shift our support to that of "experimenting is good" for business. This is where the Experimenter gift comes in!

Be a moving experiment of embracing failure and having a willingness to go for your ideas. No fear.

You are an Experimenter because you like to try new ideas. You are not afraid to experiment. You know how to experiment and how to deliver. You intuitively know when to call it quits or when to swiftly move forward. You know when to shelve experiments for a better time. You are curious about how something will come to fruition. You test many ways something could work. You are curious about the impact or results new solutions or ideas will have on the team, customer, and business. You are inclusive to ensure different perspectives are considered. You look for upstream and downstream impacts the solution or idea will have on the organization and business.

Experimentation is a gift I love to see teams use as they find innovative solutions. Those who drive this behavior and approach have the gift! They can influence others simply through the process of gathering tons of ideas, vetting them, and testing them. Then, when something doesn't come to fruition, they help the team move quickly through it with tweaks or decide to can it all together without dwelling on it. The gift brings awareness to the process of experimenting and when to call it quits, adjust, or move forward swiftly. I have found that experimentation can be a step toward a bigger change. Calling out doing a proof of concept with a subset of customers or employees before a full implementation can get more buy-in from leadership. You also have the opportunity to gather testimonials and feedback to share as part of the bigger rollout, which helps with change management.

The challenge of the Experimenter can be not delivering at all or to a timeline of expectation. One way to overcome this is to ensure you have a solid project manager or agile scrum master on a team to hold accountability for delivery. Also, communicate, communicate, communicate updates! Keep key stakeholders involved with how things are going.

Encouraging experimentation in business, education, and other industries will continue to innovate the traditional ways of solving problems, elevating society, and bringing new perspective to old conditioning.

Collaborator

Another key gift most innovators carry with them is inclusiveness. In order to bring diverse experiences, thoughts, perspectives, skills, and approaches, having a collective with this melting pot of "different" can be all that is needed to innovate quickly and significantly. Remember those one hundred or one thousand ideas needed for experimentation? It also can be done alone, and I don't want to underestimate the power of individual innovation, since much in history has come from individuals. I tend to struggle with the "let's all go to the bathroom together" approach over independence (going solo) and won't glorify group think here. I want to call out specifically what makes up being inclusive versus just "group think." Group think can still be made up of like-minded people with similar backgrounds and viewpoints which can lead to the same results. Instead, cast a net!

Be the leader who embodies nonjudgment and acts as a holder of presence, warmth, and support by creating space for others.

You are a collaborator because you think about upstream and downstream impacts to decisions, process changes, and messaging. You seek input from different perspectives. You ask the questions that challenge others to expand the viewpoint. You expand the viewpoint yourself. You invite those that get left out of the conversations to offer fresh input. You are big picture and systems thinking enough to realize future impacts now. You rally folks to be part of and not just recipients of change. You offer support in an authentic and purposeful way. You challenge status quo. Your intentions are for the impact of the solution or outcome and not for personal recognition.

My team used to call this out all the time. My first question (the challenger) when they begin working with a new project team is, "Have you looked at folks from this group, team, etc.?" Also, that ole SME (subject matter expert) is so old-school! There are so many folks who may not be considered the SME of an area or process who have even better viewpoints of solutions and even of identifying a problem. Typically, I've found SMEs (including myself) to be TOO CLOSE to the process/problem, etc., or they created that process and will hold it too close to the vest to be open to a different way of doing something. My team goes off to find the curious ones, the passionate ones, those who have experience outside of their current role, company, or even industry! We love tapping into those folks less than two to three years at the company for their ideas and drive to innovate.

A little extra to help encourage both experimentation and inclusion gifts fully includes moving past an ego-centric mindset. Here are some key ways to overcome and flow freely.

This is the paradigm shift of:

- Open heart instead of defensiveness.
- Honesty, clarity, and vulnerability instead of mixed signals or manipulation.
- Sovereignty instead of co-dependency.

- Commitment instead of trying.
- Excellence instead of perfectionism.
- Courage instead of hiding.
- Brilliance instead of settling.

Dependency of recognition, validation, and the need to prove oneself can be challenging conditioning when building your gifts of Experimenter and Inclusion. You don't need to know the answers or be the smartest person in the room to find success. Bring the collective together with an approach and process to enable success with accountability and boundaries that all agree to.

20

INFLUENCING OTHERS

*The most powerful person in the world is the storyteller. The storyteller
sets the vision, values, and agenda of an entire generation that is to come.*
——Steve Jobs

Storyteller

I have become super fond of the Storyteller gift. Storytelling is innate
to us, as that was our form of record for thousands of years. Which is
why we have a "need" to be spoken to through stories, because they
bring us into contact with our inner being. We are, in fact, storytellers
by nature. It's in everyday shares (social, reviews, bios, email, and text
messages). You hear about it in marketing content creation nowadays,
so everyone is pretty aware, but I want to dig into the "other"
storyteller. The one who influences teams, customers, and investors
with their way of taking a big picture idea and flowing effortlessly from
beginning to end of the what and why, and who can help others to
envision it's reality and be part of bringing it to life. Those who can
make the how seem simple, practical, and revolutionary. The one
whose voice and methods are essential to their way of communicating
and perceiving the world.

The Storyteller shares how a team is performing, producing, and
creating value for their customers and the company, not about the tasks,

roles/responsibilities, and results separately. They create the story that makes the team shine. They paint a picture, including the pain points. Why they decided to take ownership and how they did is what brings the entire story together. They give the actual effort life, light, and appreciation way more than just acknowledging the parts. I've had the pleasure of working with some great storytellers, metaphor creators, and business people who can simplify the complex, making it practical and real. They hold others' attention and make connections to worlds outside of their industry to helps other relate.

As a Storyteller, you make connections with the mind and the heart.

As a Storyteller, you emotionally connect with your audience or team in a relatable way. Helping others to use their internal representations to connect to the big picture is a massive benefit of storytelling. You include visual, auditory, kinesthetic, and even auditory digital. You don't just present a business plan, you make the audience a part of the vision and story. You make connections with the mind and the heart. You also tap into imagination, which is one of those creative tools we don't use enough.

I've found this gift very useful myself in presenting new business plans to gain investment, support, and approval to take forward. Just sharing components of a plan is not what will get the buy-in of others. Owning it with passion and excitement for the bigger picture impact is what builds trust. Taking the action and getting the results is what builds credibility. Knowing the fringe areas of information helps to reduce questioning and hesitation. It's all included in the story. Allen Hillery said, "When you tell a story with data, you create a shared human experience."[11] Storytellers

---

[11] Allen Hillery, "Three Reasons Why Storytelling is Important in Business" - Blog – April 25, 2019, https://alglobehopper.medium.com/three-reasons-why-storytelling-is-important-in-business-95558de6c7e3

improve decision-making through increased understanding and not solely through logic, but on a broader and more creative perspective.

The challenged side of the Storyteller may be exaggeration or going a bit too far. I love this though, as this gets people really thinking of "what's possible." Misusing the skill can be extreme, such as an exaggerator or maybe even a bit of a liar. The challenge manifests when the Storyteller can't resist making up a story to conceal something. Sometimes this is in an effort to impose order on what sometimes seems like a chaotic and random world. A possible solution is giving oneself boundaries. Read the audience so when you go off the rails, you get the cue to reel back in.

Networker

Although networking seems like a very modern skill tied to career advancement, it is actually quite ancient. The gift of the Networker is that they expand their sphere of influence by forging alliances and making connections among vastly different groups of people. This can be traced back to the Middle Ages, Greece, Rome, and ancient China. Networking would also have been an integral part of any military alliance as well as all social groups in prehistory.

Not to get religious here, but take a look at pretty much every religion/myth in the world. In almost every culture on earth, there has been a messenger of the gods who networks between the divine and human realms. This gift is not new, nor is it only relative to "work." Nowadays networking has expanded so significantly with the use of technology, social networks, and instant messaging. Making connections has become exponential. What does that really mean though? In ancient times there was effort and time invested in others. Today it's more about ourselves. Getting something we want and getting it instantly.

The Networker gift today goes further. Those with it connect personally, authentically, and not just through technology. They exchange energy, love, and gratitude. The Networker has social flexibility and empathy that enables them to find commonality with others who might not at first seem to be potential friends or allies. The Networker has the skills to bring information or power and inspiration to disparate groups of people. They choose their words wisely. They exchange only when it's worth the exchange, not just because they feel it's expected.

You are a Networker because you remove barriers to bring alignment and agreement amongst groups and people.

You are a Networker because you approach relationships from a humble and vulnerable authenticity. You are open about your intentions. You listen and genuinely engage. You show trust and build trust with those you engage. You are not demanding. You are approachable and inclusive. You are a connector to help others achieve their goals. You inquire about others instead of focusing on yourself. You remove barriers to bring alignment between groups. You leverage relationships to create solutions. You proactively exchange energy through your investment of time and conscious thought.

One of my favorite ways to see this gift shine is when I see a Networker engage another department because something needs to be solved or there is an opportunity to expand their value exchange. Instead of allowing friction, tension, or unknowns to continue, they reach out and build an understanding of how their team or organization can partner better. It's not for personal gain, but for the team, organization, customer, or company. I've also seen this between companies, when a Networker reaches out to build an understanding of how they can work better together. Again not for personal gain, but to improve experiences and value.

The challenge of the Networker is merely using others for personal gain. This could mean creating a relationship because of needing a job or working to get promoted. There is nothing wrong with this, but this is not the elevated gift I'm referring to here. The Networker may also be taken advantage of if the other person/group is engaging only for personal gain, so the Networker should be cautious.

21

REINVENTING
EXPECTATIONS

Create a vision and never let the environment, other people's beliefs, or the
limits of what has been done in the past shape your decisions.
——Tony Robbins

Influencer

Being decisive is an elevated gift. It's challenging to allow the influencer gift to flourish in a time when we are so bombarded with information and decisions. Being decisive takes "decision-making" to a totally different level—from a task to a way of being. What really makes it stand out is knowing what you want, understanding your core values, being true to your integrity, confidence, and practice. I've found being an influencer through decisiveness is pretty rare out there, which is why I've included it in the elevated gifts. It's in us, we have the tools, we just need to unlock the gift.

Being decisive saves time and emotional churn, and creates clarity for others. Knowing what you want, showing what you want, and being who you are all play a role in bringing this gift out. This is one of my gifts. I think I blew away the mind of our builder and his wife recently with my decisiveness. During a day of "picking" things out for a renovation my husband and I are doing on our house, we needed to make about twenty-five decisions from tile to shingles.

Here's the trick: I knew this day was coming. My husband and I have talked a lot about what we want style-wise and we typically are on the same page when it comes to colors, style, etc. I spent time looking at different pictures online, everything from paint to cabinets. I used a collage app to put pictures together to get an idea of the overall look. I did some work to be ready. I/we knew exactly what I/we wanted. There were tweaks to make based on what was available versus what I had found online, but we got pretty close. My decisiveness gift really came out when it came to the kitchen countertops. We started looking at a quartz and kitchen place where we found out bathroom tile, etc. (which was even better than I was originally willing to do). Then we found the best countertop options. However, the next stop was the granite place, and since quartz was more expensive, we were open to the granite. There were some beautiful slabs, but nothing hit home. Nothing compared to the quartz we found at the other shop. As we were walking around I said, "You know, this isn't going to work with the style we are trying to build. I want the quartz. We will cut costs on cupboards." I was already thinking simple shaker design anyway. Boom, done. I spoke up and it saved us at least an hour of hemming and hawing back and forth when I already knew what I wanted. There were only a couple of things that popped up that my husband and I had to decide on the spot, and it was easy and quick to make decisions.

You are a decisive influencer because you don't hem and haw about making decisions. You look forward to making decisions and getting things going.

You are a decisive influencer because you know what you want. You are clear in setting expectations. You have done your research and collected information to make informed decisions. You know your core values and prioritize and live by them daily. You believe in your self-worth. You hold yourself accountable for your decisions and live in *cause* (versus effect) as often as you can. You don't hem and haw about making decisions. You look forward to them and put energy into them. You don't shy away or view decisions as a burden. You are quick. You use your intuition along with information you have. You ask the questions you need to get to the point and make the decision.

There are a couple of different ways I see the decisive influencer gift playing out in the workplace. Minimizing chaos and fear happens when a leader is decisive and empowers their teams to be so as well. Fear creates hesitation. The unknown creates fear. This is the hurdle to overcome. The most decisive people I've seen in business make quick, informed decisions and stick to their decisions so others find confidence or comfort. They may, however, adjust the "how" something may happen. They may also determine additional decisions that need to happen and act on those too.

I love seeing people be decisive in the workplace. Especially when the tendency is waddling around and hemming and hawing until someone else makes a decision. This gift can truly help improve effectiveness and productivity. It can also increase momentum, gain buy-in faster, and get to results much sooner. Typically those who challenge status quo are pretty decisive. They bring solutions to the table while challenging old ways and step up to help make it happen (self or resources). Letting go of fear of failure and being in cause, holding yourself accountable, and doing the preparation is how to unlock this elevated gift.

One of the challenges of the Influencer gift is when you hold too firmly to a decision that isn't working out, although you have an opportunity to make an adjustment. This may be ego jumping in, so it's best to take a step back and do a double-check on your intuition. Another challenge of this gift is being impatient with others who are not decisive. You then want to make the decision for them. This is one of my challenges

I have to check in with all the time. My control comes out and I just want to make the damn decision for the other person or team. Check.

Logician

In a world that is changing at the speed of light, the time to let go of risk aversion is now. There is a great gift that I feel will help keep everyone grounded while still taking some new risks. This is the gift of Risk Intelligence practiced by the Logician. Let's define Logician using the character Sherlock Holmes characteristics including the ability to use intuition, see patterns, play devil's advocate and a knack for spotting discrepancies and irregularities. Let's define intelligence, as this will open up the fullness of this gift. *Merriam-Webster Dictionary* defines intelligence as *the ability to learn or understand or to deal with new or trying situations*: reason; also: the skilled use of reason (emphasis added). Sternberg's theory identifies three types of intelligence: *practical, creative, and analytical*. For the sake of this gift, I view ALL three of these types as relevant, not just analytical, which is what people tend to lean toward when taking risks in business.

Anyone can be a risk-taker, as it simply feels risky to do anything outside of our current comfort zone. Risk taking is individualized based on beliefs, confidence, experiences, and perspective. Basically, it's not the same for everyone. I see this in business, where a group may feel so opportunistic about something, they know it's the right thing to do. Then one person comes in with some analysis that was created in a box and beats down the idea because it's too risky. It's all perspective.

It's about balancing analysis with our emotions, structure with our creativity, and intuition with our practicality. It's also shaping the story to share with others so the big picture is easy for them to be part of decisions and to fully look at an opportunity to determine exactly "how risky" it might be. The gift of risk intelligence that the Logician has is in everyone. If you look around to so many companies who took a risk to develop a completely new channel, it's pretty obvious that the traditional, slow-moving, risk-adverse companies end up being the ones that are obsolete. This gift is one that can help to shape the future of each of us, our communities, businesses, and the world.

You are a Logician because you use your practical, creative, and analytical intelligence to determine risks.

You are a Logician because you know how to bring all aspects of a situation or opportunity into a big picture frame. You leverage all of your intelligence to make decisions. You consider data, but are not dictated only by data in making decisions. You don't shy away from risks. You like to challenge the status quo and bring ideas to the table that expand thinking. You are prepared and do your homework on all components of an idea or opportunity. You leverage all of your intelligence: analytical, creative, and practical.

Anytime we are analyzing risks we go to the data. We determine every single scenario we can think of based on the past and the thresholds of the organization or company. How far are they willing to go and how much do they have to risk? This also creates risk aversion. It's how we've always done it. Data is only a component. Adam Grant gives perspective around how and when data should be used in decisions in this post:

In a stable world, it's best to be data-driven. In a changing world, it's better to be data-informed. Data can reveal patterns from the past. It takes judgment to predict how those patterns will evolve in the future. Data shouldn't guide decisions. They should inform decisions.[12]

The challenge of the Logician can be overconfidence when the ego takes over. Check on the truth of this against your intuition. The challenge can also be swaying too far toward one of the intelligence components like analysis. Some of the intelligence is lost, as it's not a

---

[12] Adam Grant (@AdamMGrant), Twitter, July 22, 2021, https://twitter.com/AdamMGrant/status/1418217471488806912

complete evaluation or perspective. There can be a feeling of rejection, since you will be battling against many patriarchal ways of doing things that are more in the analytical. Hang in there and focus on the risks that you are truly passionate about. Eventually, your credibility will grow (as a result of other believed risks resulting in what you predicted) and others will get on board with your risks.

22

CHALLENGING THE STATUS QUO

Someone is sitting in the shade today because someone planted a tree a long time ago.
——Warren Buffett

Liberator

Think about a time when you challenged the status quo because you believed in something so deeply (possibly not even truly knowing why). Did that have an impact on those around you? Did you also see those same people challenge either a process, way of doing something, or a belief that was very outdated because of your brave lead? We are in a time where a major refresh is at play. We call it transformation or innovation, we call it a shift in leadership style or hierarchy/structure. If you have surrendered to this new age (versus fighting change), you will be able to leverage the Liberator gift you have within you to help bring new ideas to your teams, company, and community to solve not only everyday problems, but truly transform your business, company, or community by challenging old or outmoded beliefs. You will have this impact on others.

I view this gift as a proactive one. It takes action to show others that they, too, can take action. This is a very personal gift because, first and foremost, it's about liberating oneself. Awareness and acknowledging the outmoded beliefs is the first step. Being open to finding new solutions and change is what creates spark. Empowering others to do the same is what creates momentum. I'm not using the word in terms of historical reference, but rather that this is the word that comes to mind when I see this gift playing out in others. And especially the impact it has on them..

You are a Liberator because you empower others to challenge outmoded beliefs and find freedom in their passion for innovation.

You are a Liberator because you challenge the status quo of old, outmoded beliefs around process, structure, values, programs, plans, culture, etc. You get out of your comfort zone to ensure you commit to the change needed. You can shift your beliefs to support a better way. You empower others through your authenticity. You show up in a vulnerable way that gives others confidence they can too. You clearly see what and when something needs to be challenged. You bring solutions to the table to help shift the beliefs. You do not go to "that didn't work in the past." Everything has it's cycle and best timing.

In business I see this gift play out in challenging status quo and the commitment to get the self out of its comfort zone. Wanting to change the comfortable world someone may live in at work shows they are committed to following through with change. When leaders put themselves in this position, they empower others to do the same. When they show how easy it is to shift, others drop their resistance and do their thing as well. This could even be in suggesting to restructure without territory-grabbing or shielding your team from change. The Liberator gift is one that can take some heat from old believers, but it's worth the effort.

The challenges of the Liberator can lead to being forceful in challenging, the ego interfering with the authentic engagement with others, taking on everything at once and not impacting anything, not genuinely believing in what they are challenging, and challenging for the sake of challenging. The Liberator can check in with themselves to see if what they are challenging is truly the most important or desired thing to challenge at that time and the timing is the best.

Challenger

I'll start out this gift with a clarification. In my opinion, there is a difference between a questioning mindset and a Challenger. I've seen a questioning mindset go off the rails and in every single engagement or email they question why, what, who. They are posing questions to seek information more than offering value. Typically this ends up being an "expert status," ego, or self-esteem issue (validation). The questioning mindset may start out with good intentions, but can get derailed really quickly. This also causes meetings to go much longer then needed without any more of an impact to anything relevant to the conversation. So let's leave the questioning mindset at the door.

The Challenger gift not only challenges current state or decisions that may not have a big picture viewpoint, but they challenge others to "think bigger." They challenge status quo. I love this gift because "they" are the ones who get us to think about things more deeply, more broadly, and more intensely in ways we were not even considering. I also view this gift as a way to help others develop critical thinking, big-picture business assessment, creative intelligence, and problem-finding/solving—it sparks curiosity in others!

You are a Challenger. A challenger seeds visions that challenge limitations. Your gifts as a Challenger brings clarity, precision, and direction to vision. The Challenger is the clarifier of aligned and grounded higher vision and purpose on behalf of the whole.

You are a Challenger because you intentionally challenge current decisions, processes, and deliverables through different methods. This includes value questioning, offering solutions, and other straightforward approaches. You not only challenge, but offer suggestions, solutions, and help to make changes happen. You empower those around you by bringing out their abilities and gifts. You're direct, yet respectful, and bring a sense of resonance to engagements through compassion. You don't beat around the bush with fifty questions to get to the statement. You get to clarity quickly.

Just because you may make others feel uncomfortable by "asking so many questions" does not mean it's the wrong approach. It's an inclusive approach versus just telling them the answer! This gift brings an impact to not only decisions, approaches, and solutions, but it has a direct impact on others by empowering them to tap into their gifts too.

The Challenger challenges can be similar to the Liberator. Being afraid to share your ideas is the most common, which translates to not speaking up. I've heard this personally, "You are too strong in your opinions." Have you heard that one before? Yep. Just because you may be challenging something passionately does not mean you should not be allowed to pursue the opportunity. The negative impact of not allowing your gift to shine is that you dim your light. Over time this has a negative impact on your self-esteem and your contributions to your job and community. The other way the Challenger gift challenge is experienced is by excluding others you feel won't have the same viewpoints or won't accept your ideas. The issue here is that others can't help bring change to the situation and then dim their own light.

23

EMBRACE YOUR PREFERENCES

We all move along the continuum of introvert and extrovert behaviors and preferences all day long.
——Patricia Weber

Introvert + Extrovert = Ambivert

There are many myths about introverts and extroverts, and we will debunk them in this section. Extroverts don't like to be alone. All people thrive in a team environment collaborating all … day … long. Introverts don't like to be around people. Introverts don't make good leaders or public speakers. Introverts are more intellectual or creative then extroverts. It's easy to tell if someone is introverted or extroverted. I'm bringing this topic into play because, like me, many people don't understand why they have certain preferences, yet feel they have to play the game and be like everyone else.

Susan Cain, author of Quiet: The Power of Introverts in a World That Can't Stop Talking provides "A Manifesto for Introverts":

1. There's a word for "people who are in their heads too much": thinkers.

2. Solitude is a catalyst for innovation.

3. The next generation of quiet kids can and must be raised to know their own strengths.

4. Sometimes it helps to be a pretend extrovert. There will always be time to be quiet later.

5. But in the long run, staying true to your temperament is key to finding work you love and work that matters.

6. One genuine new relationship is worth a fistful of business cards.

7. It's OK to cross the street to avoid making small talk.

8. "Quiet Leadership" is not an oxymoron.

9. Love is essential; gregariousness is optional.

10. 'In a gentle way, you can shake the world.' - Mahatma Gandhi[13]

We all have different preferences for how we engage, create space, and manage our energy. The extroversion spectrum is something I learned about seven years ago from a friend when he called himself an extroverted introvert. I thought, "Wow, that's what I am too." I started doing research and found an interesting world of preferences. I also found it a necessary thing to appreciate what others need and prefer that may be different from me.

Yes, I was a shy girl growing up and typically didn't speak up. When I tell folks I'm engaged with that I'm more of an introvert naturally, they look at me like I have two heads. Mainly because I am not afraid to speak my mind and share my thoughts with them freely. I come across as what a perceived extrovert would be. However, as I did my research many years ago, I found there are very different preferences that introverts and extroverts have.

Traditionally, we only assume a shy person is introverted and a social person is an extrovert. There are many preferences that each have that will

---

[13] Susan Cain, The Power of Introverts, https://www.thepowerofintroverts.com/sixteen-things-i-believe

throw this out the generalization window. As I did my research, took quizzes, and had conversations with others, the realization came to light that this is a big and important piece to understanding and accepting ourselves and each other. I also started adjusting my expectations of my team based on their preferences. Instead of a cookie-cutter expectation, I tuned in with them more intently.

I also realized my own tendencies to "need" alone time and energy drains from being around people were introverted tendencies and a part of who I am. Yet, I can turn it on when I need to, which shows more extroverted tendencies. I've been called "intense" (yes many, many times), extremely focused (including not even hearing my mother ask me to do the dishes while watching TV when I was young), always thinking, and passionate! Believe it or not, all of these characteristics are actually introverted. I came to the conclusion that I was also an extroverted introvert.

What's interesting is that it's not as much of a "tendency" as a preference, and even a need. In the technology industry there are MANY of us with stronger introverted tendencies and qualities. Why is it important to know what our needs and preferences are and of those around us? We will drive each other crazy otherwise, or force unrealistic expectations of our own preferences upon others in a damaging and/or unproductive way. We may also be standoffish or overwhelming to others without realizing it.

During our Exploratory Lab Boot Camp for college students many years ago, there was a student who self-proclaimed he was an introvert, and it prompted a conversation about what is important to introverts. This was intriguing to me, as two expectations of the boot camp are working in a collaborative group and networking with potential employers. At the end of June that year we hosted another Exlab Boot Camp and had a wonderful group of students (ages 19–50) participate. As I opened the boot camp I made a point to call myself out as an introvert or, more precisely, an extroverted introvert.

What I didn't realize was the incredible impact that public proclamation made on one student's entire week! At the end of the week he shared with me very intentionally how that one statement broke down his own barriers and walls, and a sense of freedom opened up a week of possibilities and comfort.. He IS an introvert, yet he typically represented his group in sharing solutions, ideas, and decisions that his team came up with during activities throughout the week, and he was very open about what caused him challenges in "networking," as well as the exhaustion he felt from being so engaged all week.

Assessment—It's time to take a quick assessment, if you are interested. Then you will completely understand the remaining message! This assessment takes less than five minutes. Where do you fall on the extroversion spectrum? This is just one website where you can take the test and find out, quietrev.com. Heads up, you will be asked to provide your email address.

Introvert—I like getting my energy from dealing with the ideas, pictures, memories, and reactions that are inside my head, in my inner world. I often prefer doing things alone or with one or two people I feel comfortable with. I take time to reflect so that I have a clear idea of what I'll be doing when I decide to act. Ideas are almost solid things for me. Sometimes I like the idea of something better than the real thing.

Here is a quick overview of characteristics of an introvert:
- Energized by inside world
- Prefer alone time, solitude
- Focused
- Self-aware
- Prefer email, text, and social communications over phone and face-to-face
- Intuitive

- Energized by passion for a topic/activity
- Deliberate approach to risk
- Think before speaking
- Recharge by being alone
- Introspective thinkers
- Reflective
- Prefer to create by themselves and are creative
- Prefer small groups closest to them
- Overwhelmed in loud, crowded settings
- Being with people drains their energy

Extrovert—I like getting my energy from active involvement in events and having a lot of different activities. I'm excited when I'm around people and I like to energize other people. I like moving into action and making things happen. I generally feel at home in the world. I often understand a problem better when I can talk out loud about it and hear what others have to say.

Here's an overview of characteristics of an extrovert:

- Energized by the world around them
- Enjoy social life
- Active and hearty
- Prefer phone calls and face-to-face
- Likes variety
- Expressive
- Speak as they think
- Typically assertive and are go-getters
- Think on their feet
- Prefer stimulating environments
- Comfortable with conflict
- Enjoy seeing and speaking with others
- Being alone drains their energy

So how many of your assessments came back as ambivert? Wait, what is this? Ambiverts have preferences in the best of both worlds. They float back and forth on the extroversion spectrum, depending on situations and settings. Typically work settings will draw out more of their extroverted side, but they are still deep thinkers and enjoy being in their own world. Ambiverts are compassionate and can come across as "people people." They are typically very genuine in their engagements with others.

Ambivert—I enjoy being around people, but they exhaust me, so I need to recharge. I enjoy solitude, but not for too long. I live in my world of my thoughts, visions, and ideas, although I'll share them with you. I will take risks, but with a game plan to get out, if needed. I can focus intensely to complete a project or task. My passion energizes me.

Here's an overview of characteristics of an ambivert:

- Tap into strengths of both introverts and extroverts
- Need solitude to recharge
- Outgoing on their own terms
- Very self-aware
- Sometimes speak before thinking, but other times think before speaking
- Prefer email, text, and social sites over phone and face-to-face (phone calls are special)
- Need balance or get moody
- Confusing to others
- Highly intuitive
- Empathetic to others' emotions
- Flexible, but can be indecisive
- Can work alone or in groups
- Take charge or step down, depending on situation

Did this hit home for you? In a nutshell, introverts work better alone, enjoy intimate drinks, email communication, are tired after socializing, are good writers, and are easily distracted. Extroverts like big parties, using the phone over email, are team workers, good speakers, get crowd euphoria, and are easily bored.

I also found the ambivert, which is when we float between an extrovert and introvert. Bingo, that is where I fall. I float back and forth.

Following intense collaborations, engagements, events, networking, etc., I just want to hide in my office and not talk to anyone! You may think this is unacceptable, but I desperately feel the need to get into my own world, focus intensely, knock out my to-do list, and not engage with anyone! I'm exhausted. I need to recharge, and based on how fast-paced and intense things can get, I may need a couple of days to do so. That doesn't mean I'm not working my ass off, because it actually ends up being my most productive time!

I know this about myself, and I will tell folks this so they understand my in and out behavior and not take it personally. I will block my calendar, take a long weekend, or work remote to help me recharge. I also have to get outdoors to camp, hike, or just take a walk every so often. Nature recharges me, and I know it does.

Quick Exercise

Think through each scenario below and jot down your answers. These are things you can use to boost your energy or at least manage it more effectively, regardless of which end of the spectrum you tend to prefer more.

1. Who energizes you?
   o You get excited being around them.
   o They instill confidence in you.
   o They are helpful and complimentary.
   o They allow you to share your ideas in a nonthreatening environment.
   o You feel energized around them.
2. Who drains you?

- o You tense up.
- o You don't enjoy being around them.
- o You are exhausted after engaging with them.
- o You hate the thought of engaging with them.
- o Hearing their name makes you feel exhausted.
- o They decrease your confidence.

Engage as much as you can handle with folks who energize you! Spend time, engage, and include them in your world. I have different groups of ladies I work on community projects with whom I get so much energy from just being around. They are my crack!

If you are around folks who just drain you, try these tips and/or try to minimize your time with them. Choose settings, environments, time of day, and amount of time when you can handle them best and when you have time before and after the engagement to charge and recharge yourself!

Managers shouldn't treat everyone the same, and that includes the extroverts on your team. You can, however, be conscientious of settings, meetings, expectations to engage, how to include introverts, and build an environment where both ends of the spectrum, as well as the ambiverts, thrive—or at least enjoy!

What's important to introverts:

- Space
  - o Respect of their personal space
  - o 1:1 conversations
  - o Ability to be quiet without repercussions
  - o Avoiding loud, crowded places
- Energy
  - o Recharging frequently
  - o Avoiding wasted energy
  - o Escaping too much talking
  - o Space and time to recharge

- Avoiding exhaustion from overstimulation
- Inclusion
  - Feeling included
  - Freedom to choose whether to attend a social event without pressure
  - Time to think
- Creation
  - Personal time to create, which sparks passion and energy
  - Living in their world and in their head
  - Avoiding forced collaboration in groups

What's important to extroverts:
- Engagement
  - Offered options
  - Understanding of their busy times
  - Exploring and talking things out
  - Social events
- Energy
  - Making physical and verbal gestures of affection
  - Letting them speak to think
  - Allowing them to multitask
  - Working in stimulating environments
- Inclusion
  - Acceptance and encouragement of their enthusiasm
  - Letting them dive right in
  - Respecting their independence
  - Group discussions
- Attention
  - Complimenting them in the company of others
  - Letting them shine

- o   Thoughtfully surprising them
- o   Listening to their many ideas

You can pick and choose the items important to you from each list if you were assessed as an ambivert. Share your preferences with others. Embrace them! You will find a freedom in this exercise to really being able to show up as your authentic self and bring your elevated gifts to the table, while also supporting others on their journey.

Work Process and Style

So much has the opportunity to change, and we have the opportunity to make the changes to embrace a healthier and happier life. One of the preferences to consider is your working style. Most people work shift jobs or eight a.m.to five p.m. schedules that are not flexible, but there are many jobs that can be challenged for their "structured" work hours, location, and engagement style. I've had many members on my teams over the years who have openly stated they work better in the afternoons and at night, or have to pick up children in the afternoon to transport them to after-school care. I've also had many members enjoy working in their space of choice. The pandemic proved that remote working is absolutely effective and that, if companies have the right systems in place with aligned goals and trust of their employees, they can feel confident in their workforce. Getting the job done and getting to results is the ultimate goal, whether in a centralized structure (office) or elsewhere (home, Starbucks, co-op space, etc.).

I made a statement as companies were starting to open their offices back up that I was not going to reinstate my commute, and we made the move to live where we want, not where my office was located. I was willing to go into the office when absolutely needed, but my team was decentralized across multiple states anyway, so it didn't make sense to force people into a specific office location. The amount of energy left from my day when I didn't have to commute three to four hours a day changed my everything - lifestyle, health, habits (cooking healthier), and sleep. I know I'm not the only one who wanted to hold onto these benefits of working remote and having flexibility. Companies should not force people back into offices just because they own buildings/properties or are stuck in the old world of having to have an office and thinking that is how culture is curated. Culture is healthy when culture is healthy, and that's up to the leaders and employees. That's based on everything I've shared in part 1.

Of course, there are many people who want to go back to an office setting. They enjoy physical engagement versus video/phone/email and get their energy from that setting. I felt that I was closer to my team when we were all remote than previously. We set scheduled time to engage on nonwork topics to get to know each other better and to hold space for our relationship. Previously, the folks in the office would have hallway conversations or over-the-cube chats, but others were left out who weren't in the office. Most of the chats were work-related anyway, so the personal connection wasn't as deep as we ended up forming over video calls when we were all remote.

Regarding work hours, glorifying working more than your committed time is not healthy, nor does it really get you anything. I can remember a time when I was working sixty to eighty hours a week for over a year and only sleeping about three hours a night. I was at my most unhealthy and least happy in my life. While I felt I had to do this to turn around a business and team, I decided at one point it was insane. I made changes, and empowered team members who were stepping into bigger roles and skills. I shifted some of the expectations and came back to reality.

In quite a few chapters I wrote about getting rid of nonessential tasks and solo-tasking where you can, and simplifying your processes. Focusing on one task at a time deeply and quickly is what I call solo-tasking. This will help you reduce how many hours you have to put in to get to the same or better results.

I've found over the years that I can actually do my job in less time than most (not to brag, it's just a superpower) because I didn't mess around. My capacity is high, so I'm able to shift and take on more. I can stay focused even with a hurricane blowing through the room. So my output is high. I work a lot in my head after hours and put fingers to keyboard to create those thoughts. I don't believe in a forty-hour, eight a.m. to five p.m. work-week structure anymore. I also don't believe we should work a forty-hour work week anymore, and I don't. This is an old patriarchal and industrial way of working which does not match the times, technology, globalization, or human behavior. Businesses can be up and running twenty-four hours a day, and people can buy in that same time frame. So how does a forty-hour work week still apply?

My current schedule is that on Monday's I run my business, create, and plan. I offer podcast interview slots and coaching sessions in the afternoon. On Tuesdays, Wednesdays, and Thursdays I offer one or the other or both in the afternoons, and I don't work on Fridays. Depending on the week, I work about twenty hours. If I have a special project or inspiration I want to create, I may work more. If I have fewer appointments, I work less.

Freelance jobs have a similar type of flexibility. I meet with clients during the day, but if you are an early bird or a night owl, you typically work during those hours that make sense for your working preference. It's important to note that there are many more freelance jobs out there. Many folks work these on the side to build a client base or for extra income. It's great to team up with someone who has a specialty, especially if you are an entrepreneur. I always say, outsource what you can and focus on where you bring value.

The last topic I want to cover here is on the working process or creative process. I used to think I was a procrastinator, because I'd wait until the last minute to create a presentation, book report, or any output with a message and information. It took me until my forties to realize that it was just part of my creative process. It wasn't that I didn't start until then. I would just take my creation and shove it into a tool to deliver it at the end. I work in my head a lot as my introverted side clearly displays. During moments when I have a few minutes (or schedule time to think), I will research, ask questions, get input from others, and toss around ideas in my head for potentially weeks ahead. I'll form the creation in my head first before getting it into a visual message for others via PowerPoint, video, or other tools to deliver to an audience. That is not procrastination, it's my creative process. It was honestly a relief to realize this, and I not only stopped beating myself up about "procrastinating," I now embrace my process and deeply connect with it as a great method for me. I listen to my "muses" and let the ideas flow.

24

BALANCE - OUR BEST WAY TO BRING OUT OUR GIFTS

Harmonized leadership alchemizes all of our strengths by integrating the feminine principles of cooperation, love, receptivity, vulnerability, tenderness, spontaneity, beauty, connection, and inclusion with the masculine principles of focused direction, divine order, humble decisiveness, honorable discipline, and passionate purpose.
——Elayne Kalila *Doughty*

Strategy and Execution

There is so much pressure to be strategic, think bigger, be creative, and meet expectations. When strategy and execution are out of balance, we tend to be working harder than is necessary. Finding balance between strategy and execution is important in your work life. It provides a sense of being purposeful, and you see the results without forcing them. There is an opportunity to redefine "strategy" so it resonates more with everyone. According to the *Oxford English Dictionary*, it's defined as "a plan of action or policy designed to achieve a major or overall aim." This sounds so basic and easy, yet expectations of strategy in the workplace tend to miss the point of "plan of action" and hover more around actual vision. This is where the disconnect happens and where many get left behind. They are left behind because they feel they are expected to create a new business model or solution that brings in more business.

Let's go with a new definition. Strategy is a step to design how you will achieve a goal. This is something people can relate to. They can be strategic in their day-to-day and use their creativity to design their plan of action. Strategy is about the how. This is left out of many conversations in the workplace, with everyone just making assumptions and creating theories about "how" to be strategic. Many folks can be strategic, but lack knowing how to execute something. There are so many "titles" today that have the word strategy in them, yet they can be so disconnected from the greater picture of achieving the goals set out.

Execution is a strength for many. It is "what" needs to be done today, tomorrow, and the next day to get closer to achieving the goal. They didn't necessarily design the action plan, but they are carrying it out. They are adjusting where needed to make the strategy come to life. They may even bring feedback to the table that shows the strategy needs to be adjusted. Is anyone listening? Where roles really hinder gifts is slotting some employees in the execution box without showing them how to be strategic and shoving others in the strategy box without holding them accountable to execution.

Balance comes when strategy and execution are closely tied together and in balance. Structure, goals, and accountability should be shared and skill-building around both should be expected. This allows for more elevated gifts to come out and be appreciated. This also creates a collaboration of intention and aligned outcomes. Authentic vulnerability sharing that the strategy just isn't working or the execution is failing should be appreciated for its role in achieving success.

Feminine and Masculine Energy

In this section we are going deeper into how to find balance in ourselves between our feminine and masculine qualities. Here is a quick reference for perspective. Examples of masculine qualities include directive, decisive, disciplined, purposeful, initiator, orderly, logical, rational, and goal-oriented. Examples of feminine qualities include cooperation, love, receptivity, relation, balance, vulnerability, tenderness, spontaneity, collaboration, inclusion, empathy, humility, generosity, beauty, connection, and nurturing. I'm going to call it that to bring awareness to this topic specifically. Yes, they both exist in each of us. It's not a gender thing, it's a human thing. It's also about embracing each and both when it best fits the situation. THIS is the gift we each have! Given the tendency to traditionally embrace masculine qualities in our patriarchy for thousands of years, it's about finally embracing a balance of both. This is the gift. You may have seen success in situations when both are felt and used appropriately and in balance. Integrating the two gives us focused direction, humble decisiveness, honorable discipline, balanced view, patient strategy, and passionate purpose.

Here is the backdrop of why I find this topic not only interesting, but crucial as we move forward together as a society and as humans, and why I want to share. A few years ago I found myself burned-out, overwhelmed, and completely over-tasked! Yes, I am a taskmaster and feel the need to organize everything. Call it control, call it perfectionism, or call it crazy. Yes, crazy! Not a healthy way to live and not necessary. I literally felt my energy drained from me every day.

So, I sought out an energy worker. I found a fantastic one in St. Petersburg, Florida and immediately started working with her. Our first session found my masculine energy (held physically in the right side of our body) not only throughout my right side, but most of the bottom left part of my body. I was only holding feminine energy from my heart up and out of my head. Ok, hang with me in case this is all new to you. Not only did I feel my energy out of whack, but it literally was completely out of balance. We did some work to help tune up my energy and it was amazing. I worked with Ashley for many months in many ways that has helped me to better understand "why" I allowed this to happen and how to keep myself from getting out of balance again. Because it does happen, and often.

I've also done a ton of research and participated in classes/groups to better understand how this happens and how to stay in balance. Now I literally can feel when I'm heading out of balance and I take action; I meditate, focus on an alternative approach, and deliberately do things (not my normal conditioning) to find balance. It's an ongoing awareness and process. This includes both home and work life.

It also has led me down the path of simplifying my life and not overcommitting or stretching myself like I previously felt I "had" to do to be purposeful. Now I make decisions that intuitively are best for my mind, body, and spirit. I have to say that the Covid experience of slowing down and going inside was an enabler to give me the freedom and personal permission to keep my new lifestyle and habits, which I'm so grateful for. I'm not giving it up for anything!

I've found that this is critical to ensuring you are able to open up all of your other elevated gifts as well. You can specifically bring awareness to the "what" and "how" you are leading your day and using your energy, and take action to keep your masculine and feminine qualities in balance.

There are a few specific options to consider in situations as alternative ways to use your gifts. The desire many have in the business world and world in general vary from traditional supposed expectations, behaviors, and conditioning. Why does this matter? Because the more we embrace a balance, the more authentic we are, the happier and more effective we will be together, in our lives, with our families, in our communities, with our teams, and in our jobs. Let's dive in!

Cooperation Over Competition

Competition is something we are conditioned with from even before we can remember whether it's deliberate or just part of our language, in comparison to others or learning how to "set goals" from a young age. I've seen so much of this in the workplace over my twenty-seven-year career in corporate environments, felt it, and have also been competitive at times. There is a time and place for it for sure, but it shouldn't be 100 percent of everything we do and who we are. Try this for a change: cooperation. In the most recent years, many "personality tests" done in the workplace have identified cooperation as somewhat of a negative trait. Cooperation does not mean "giving up or in." It's not weakness, it's effectiveness. It moves conversations along to action and creates trust, as well as partnership, when necessary. I think if there was more cooperation with competition, we would accomplish much more together.

Collaboration Over Force

This is a tough one. We live in such a fast-paced and goal-oriented place that, so often, we see force used not only in decisions, but in actions. Taking time to collaborate brings more ideas to the table and provides for better advocacy and change management. Decisions can still be made as appropriate whether participative/facilitative, consultative (leveraging a group or individual), delegation, or just making the decision (authoritative). Forcing our agendas, objectives, or ideas anymore really stands out. If this is a typical tactic, think about how to stop, listen, and collaborate with others. It may actually turn your idea into an even better and more well-received one while including others on the journey.

Relationship Over Territory

I have this strong belief in respect for others' property. Most wars throughout history were all about taking land, resources, riches, thrones, freedom, and will. This has created untrusting boundaries to separate us from each other. We continue this mentality in protecting our "territory" in the workplace, whether that is our area of responsibility, team, strategy, or ideas we claim as ours. Most of this is protecting ourself and ego or validating our purpose. Wars still exist unnecessarily inside of companies. If we considered relationships as more important in more instances than "our territory," it would be amazing what could not only get accomplished, but the trust that could emerge along with an open mind to new ways of doing things (like structure, responsibilities, etc.).

Responsiveness Over Strategy

Having a strategy is great as long as nothing changes from the day you set that strategy in stone. Given the speed at which everything changes and truly not having all of the answers when we set strategy, why not approach it a bit differently? I've always used a combination of experience, input, analysis, data, AND my intuition throughout my career. More and more I hear we should only make decisions and plans using data-driven insights. Forget that ole intuition, which is a natural-born gift to everyone. How successful has that approach actually been? Leaders who have been able to assess how effective strategy has been relayed, received, and resulted before the BIG RED flags show up find more success. They and their teams flow versus holding to specific agreements in the strategy and trying to control outcomes by responding along the way. This responsive approach to change and feedback, continuous experimentation, and evaluation ends up providing success. Be open, listen, and release control.

Process Over Goal

We are a goal-oriented society taught from a young age that we need to have goals to achieve anything. We need goals in business to deliver and incent others to get to the result. Instead, why not ensure the best process is in place, which ultimately delivers the goal? Goals are good for setting a direction, but taking action through processes is best for making progress. Many problems can occur when spending too much time setting goals and not enough time on designing the best process. It's a shift in emphasis when we talk about goals. For example, determining the best process to deliver excellent customer experience is how the goal gets achieved and not just by merely setting a goal. This is where finger-pointing comes into play along with an inconsistent experience. Look at how customer experience at so many companies has floundered significantly during Covid adjustments. This is from a bad process not just lack of people working it.

Finding the balance between goals and "how" those goals get achieved ultimately provides the best solution.

Emotion and Intuition Over Thought and Logic

It's not a new concept that emotions drive human behavior over logic. Emotion has been given the "four letter word" label in business. A passionate person is emotional, emotions stir things up, emotions are not fact, emotions can't be controlled, and women can be emotional. So what? Really, this is a natural gift we as humans have and why is it bad to use emotion along with logic? Emotion is how our intuition is shared. How many thoughts do we have that are not fact either? Most of them—assumptions, judgments, and theories—we think of daily. Emotions are not just about how we feel. They are expressions and physical signals letting us know that, as humans, we should react or respond to something we just saw, heard, or felt. Finding the balance between or the time to use emotion and intuition over thought and logic is how we connect with each other.

So how hard is it to utilize both our masculine and feminine qualities in balance? It's a continuous awareness that takes both courage and support of each other.

25

BE PRESENT

Never dim your light because others are too afraid to come out of the dark.

——Matshona Dhilwayo

Mindfulness

Mindfulness is one of the most important ways I've found balance in myself. Mindfulness is a bit different then mindset, so I'll share a definition to start us out. According to the Lexico powered by *Oxford*, there are two definitions: (1) the quality or state of being conscious or aware of something, and (2) a mental state achieved by focusing one's awareness on the present moment, while calmly acknowledging and accepting one's feelings, thoughts, and bodily sensations. Karen Young describes mindfulness as "a moment-by-moment awareness of thoughts, feelings, and sensations. The idea is to allow thoughts, feelings, and sensations to come and go, without judgment or the need to do anything with them."[14] This is whole body and not just about our mind. That is what I've found to be so important to finding balance within.

---

[14] Karen Young, "13 Different Ways to Practice Mindfulness - And the Difference it Can Make"- https://www.heysigmund.com/different-ways-to-practice-mindfulness/

There are many benefits to mindfulness that can help relieve stress by improving emotion regulation, treating heart disease, lowering blood pressure, increasing resilience, improving inhibition abilities, improving concentration and memory, improving decision making, increasing job satisfaction, enhancing job performance, decreasing burnout, promoting neuroplasticity, reducing physical pain by focusing on it less, strengthening mental health, reducing depression, improving sleep quality, reducing fatigue, and alleviating gastrointestinal difficulties.[15]

What is neuroplasticity? Neuroplasticity is defined by the *Oxford English Dictionary* as the ability of the brain to form and reorganize synaptic connections, especially in response to learning or experience or following injury. It's more newly discovered that our brain can actually continue to develop as an adult. Whenever we complete a new task or find a more effective way to do something, our brain takes note, often making structural or connection changes to facilitate our next attempt at this task.

Further, when we practice mindfulness, we send the message to our brain that we are more effective at dealing with everyday tasks when we are aware, observant, nonreactive, and nonjudgmental. This causes our brain to make the changes that will improve our ability to function mindfully. There are certain areas of the brain that physically change our brain! Many studies have resulted in better understanding how the prefrontal cortex, the hippocampus, and other areas experienced heightened activity and connectivity, while the amygdala experienced decreased functional activity. This means that the areas of the brain associated with higher-level functioning were more active, while the area of the brain that handles stress and strong emotions was less involved. These findings match up with feedback and behavior changes seen after a mindfulness practice has

---

[15] Courtney E. Ackerman, "23 Amazing Health Benefits of Mindfulness for Body and Brain." *PositivePsychology.com* March 17, 2021, https://positivepsychology.com/benefits-of-mindfulness/

been implemented. There is better emotion regulation, better performance on tasks, and less reactivity.

Think about how many things in your day happen without you even realizing you are doing them (this could even be driving into the office!). Do you scarf down your meal because you view it only as fuel versus a sensory enjoyment? I have always been a fast eater. Especially once I started having children. Eating became a necessity to stay alive, fuel for my body. The faster I could finish that task, the sooner I could move on to the next thing. Sigh. I've realized not only is this habit bad for my health, but it's not a great experience in my human body.

What are ways we can practice mindfulness?[16] There are many ways you can practice mindfulness throughout your day. Some things can be done in an intentional moment and some things can be structured to build habits.

Mindful waking. Starting out your day with mindfulness sets the tone for the day. Engaging your day's purpose when you wake up is a great way to connect to what will be your intention for the day. This gets the higher centers of your brain like your prefrontal cortex activated versus your lower brain centers, which are faster, unconscious impulses.

Mindful eating. I have senses I didn't even use in the way I used to eat. Now I slow down and enjoy the taste, texture, and smell of my food. I show appreciation for its growth and preparation. I eat more mindfully. It's a conscious thing, though. Breaking any habit is not easy, so being intentional in my mindful eating is the key.

Mindful pause. According to *Mindful.org*, you can rewire your brain simply by pausing before reacting. In order to shift from the busy, autopilot habits and behaviors our neural networks support, we can stimulate neuroplasticity. Instead of relying on the shortcuts our brain has

---

[16] Parneet Pal, Carley Hauck, Elisha Goldstein, Kyra Bobinet, and Cara Bradley, "5 Simple Mindfulness Practices for Daily Life." *Mindful.org* https://www.mindful.org/take-a-mindful-moment-5-simple-practices-for-daily-life/

created for us to speed through life, we can slow things down. Shifting the balance to give your slow brain more power is the secret. Instead of autopilot, set up "if this, then that" messages to create easy reminders to shift into slow brain. I've started this practice in purchases I make, as well as activities I do for the day. If I spend time on this task, then I won't have as much time for cooking. If I wait until this afternoon to do this task, then I'll have more time to focus on it. If I get up earlier, then I'll be able to add in a yoga sequence. Instead of just tackling tasks as they come into your mind, create a little story around them. This can help to create new patterns.

Mindful workout. Exercise has not been a thing for me at all. Throughout my life I just didn't enjoy it, and always have an issue getting started and sticking to it. I make every excuse in the book to avoid it. It's because I don't enjoy traditional exercise. Aha! I love to dance and can burn off more calories doing that than walking on a treadmill. I enjoy kayaking and walking/hiking. I enjoy yoga. These are finds later in life that have inspired me. I recently found Kinrgy, which incorporates dance and aerobic exercise into an intentional connecting (elements) that is super fun and a kick-butt workout. It's live or online, and I can do it anytime. I had to break out of the traditional definition of exercise and shift my mindset to movement. These are much more mindful workouts versus going through the motions at a gym. The more you can connect your mind, body, and spirit in your movement practice, the more you activate all of the mindful benefits while moving your body.

Mindful walking. I love this practice and have a new appreciation for connecting to my environment. Some use this practice as nature walking or meditation. Again, this is about using your senses. While walking what do you see, hear, and feel? Listen to your surroundings without headphones. Look at your surroundings versus only thinking about the goal of finishing your walk. Walk different paths, areas, and distances to have a different experience. Doing this daily has a significant impact on your mindfulness in other areas. It increases your awareness and experience.

Mindful tasks. I've started to really appreciate using a broom. I mean for sweeping—ha! Mindful sweeping not only cleans the floor, but actually helps to release emotions through movement. I used to think of sweeping (or mopping) as a chore with no value other than a clean floor. I now look forward to sweeping the floor and take my time enjoying the process of release. You can take this concept to washing dishes, folding laundry, or other chores that would otherwise be mundane.

Mindful presence. We rarely make eye contact, even when someone is talking to us, or we are looking at our phone. We are thinking about other things we need to do or creating our response. Being present is challenging with all of our distractions. When my husband said to me, "You are the 'give me a minute girl,'" I took it to heart. I always had to finish what I was doing in the minute so I could fully engage. Instead, I was pushing off the opportunity to be present. I'm still working on this one, but it makes such a difference to be mindfully present, listen with intent, and engage fully with someone sitting in front of us and wanting us to engage.

Mindful meditation. I used to be so frustrated with meditation. Mainly because I thought it had to be a certain way and my mind just wouldn't slow down. What I've found is guided meditations work great for me, and I may only be able to meditate for five minutes. And that's OK. It takes consistent practice, and that's what is most important. One great benefit I've learned from meditation that helps me in my mindfulness shift is allowing thoughts to float on by instead of dissecting each of them. They are only thoughts and not all are deserving of some kind of analysis. Using this as a starting point will also give you a great way to gain mindfulness.

Mindful enjoyment. When life was crazy, even my most enjoyable hobbies, events, or activities seemed like a chore. I allowed the fast-paced, always-moving expectation to take over everything. This included what I most enjoyed. Now, I've learned to give enough time to those things I really enjoy including reading, sitting on the dock, and gardening. I don't rush them. I engage fully—mind, body, and spirit—and use all of my senses. I've found much more enjoyment in designating the space and time instead of "fitting them in" around everyone/thing else.

Mindful self-care. I used to be so disconnected from what I needed and focused on everyone/everything else around me that I didn't listen to my body. My self-care practice not only includes rest when my body says, "Slow the hell down, I'm tired," but things I enjoy like taking care of my skin (which is a ritual in and of itself). I also am aware of boundaries I need to set including saying "no," sticking to what I'm committed to, not adding anything else unless something goes away, availability to help others versus being available to everyone at all times, and tough conversations when I'm ready to engage and not based only on someone else's agenda/need.

Mindfulness is a great practice you can include in your existing daily activities. These are only some examples of things to do, but there are so many others. As you become aware of the opportunities in your day to practice, you will find many other great ways to engage your senses, body, mind, and emotions without judgment and in full experience.

Rounding Out Part 2

Finding balance through permission to use your gifts is the first step! Not just at home or in your community, but in the workplace. Realizing your difference is around embracing your elevated gifts and using them to bring change. Bringing your full authentic self to the workplace is liberating, and the freedom you find can be eye-opening to whether your environment truly matches up with your core values and true self.

If you are not accepted for who you are, is it the right environment for you?

I know you have felt the spark and resonated with many of the elevated gifts in this chapter. Laying up the foundational tools, mindset, and energy to activate those gifts will be a fantastic journey for you to embark on. These are only the elevated gifts I highlighted here, but I'm sure you will find others you embrace in yourself and others. Be open to them; they will shine through. In part 3 we will walk through activating our gifts. I'm excited you are still on this journey with me, and look forward to sharing ideas on how you can bring out your elevated gifts and share them with the world.

PART THREE
ACTIVATING YOUR
GIFTS

26

WHO ARE YOU?

Strong people have a strong sense of self-worth and self-awareness; they don't need the approval of others.
——Roy T. Bennett

Sense of Self

Let's dive into identity as we define it in the workplace. Identity is important, as it helps us to show up in the world a certain way and can and will change throughout life as our lives evolve. There are many identities we take on in life including son/daughter, mother/father, child/adult, wife/husband, leader/follower, married/divorced/single, caregiver, no identity, work identity, superhero identity—and the list can go on and on for those we "take on." I'm going to dive in over the next few sections on the challenges we have with our sense of self: self-worth, self-awareness, and a few identities surrounding work that can impact and limit us in our identity at different stages.

Sense of self is something that grounds us in who we are. It's what guides us each day and what we each have ownership of and the opportunity to improve and evolve. Before we jump into sense of self, let's define it. Your *sense of self* refers to your perception of the collection of characteristics that *define* you. Personality traits, abilities, likes and dislikes, your belief system or moral code, and the things that motivate you—these all contribute to *self-image* or your unique *identity* as a person.

Sense of self can go deeper for some who live from their inner self or for others who live from the ego. It's important either way, and neither way is right or wrong. It's really about understanding this key piece of yourself and how outside influencers can shift. Perception can be impacted by our environment and influence our personality, beliefs, and even our likes and dislikes. It can go deep and be impacted by limiting beliefs. There is so much conditioning throughout our journey from childhood to adulthood, and it continues throughout adulthood with exposure to new experiences and environments. Much of this conditioning is very limiting to how we value ourselves.

Limiting beliefs are those nasty little conditions that hold us back. I'll dive deeper into limiting beliefs in the work setting in the mindset chapter, but I'd like to introduce the impact of limiting beliefs here as we dive into sense of self. Many of our limiting beliefs were observed, shared by others, or unintentionally imprinted on us. This could be around money, career, relationships, marriage, dreams, and self-esteem.

The underlying fears of limiting beliefs are the root causes that hold us back. Fear of failure, fear of success, fear of not being good enough, fear of rejection, and fear of not being loved are the most common. If you think about a time when you started self-sabotaging because of a fear of success, you know this is a real and common issue in the workplace. Some examples include not going for a promotion, not sharing an idea that gives you credibility, etc. Typically, when we dive into the root of why we hold back, the root cause is a fear of success. Over the years I've been in so many of what I call situational mentor sessions where women have talked about their hesitation about going for a manager role, for example. The reason? The perception that with success comes a fear of more work, expectations of spending less time with family, and more stress. When we addressed these underlying fears, the mentee had a totally different perspective and would typically make their move.

The impact on how we perceive our own abilities can swing if we don't have a strong sense of self. The influence others have on how we view ourselves, and even what we like or dislike, can shift our sense of self. Having a lack of sense of self can lead to many other confidence and self-esteem issues. An environment where we can't bring our authentic self to work can negatively impact our sense of self. When this happens, a person can feel disconnected from their true self. This can also lead to taking on an identity that does not align with a person's sense of self.

The amount of energy it takes to wear a mask or identity that is not authentic can be exhausting. It can also cause shifts in the person's true belief system and even personality over time. I've seen this in others, and I've experienced this myself. Over time, losing sight of the things that motivate us will cause numbing out, which we will address in a couple of chapters. There is a distinct separation of our physical, emotional, and mental self. This can lead to feeling stuck in a rut, distancing from others, and even depression. Our sense of self is so important as a foundation to stay connected to. This is not selfish, it's necessary. Knocking out the fears and staying connected to self is our journey.

How we value ourself is living in authenticity and that means 24–7, outside of work and inside of work. When we perceive an environment as not safe to be our authentic self, we make adjustments and determine what we need to say and do and who we need to be in order to be accepted, respected, and even keep our job. It can be a stressful situation and end up causing behaviors that are not true to who we are. Then we shame ourselves for those behaviors and we question our sense of self. It's a downward spiral. Many times we struggle to stop the spiral and feel trapped in the box.

A message for leaders: instead of putting pressure on employees to fit in a box and mirror or match "you" or a labeled high-performer, ask if they are OK and how you can help. Sometimes, a simple acknowledgment they are human and you care opens up the quick turnaround the employee needs to get back to "themselves."

I've been obsessed with personality tests over the past decade. I find them a great input at least, and an aha! moment at most. Personality tests can showcase style, preferences, engagement, and opportunities to leverage knowledge to work in a responsive versus reactive mode. If you are in the box and struggling with your sense of self, here are a couple of exercises that may help. I'll dive a bit deeper in part 3 of this book, but am making a recommendation to try one here.

Make the Shift

To increase self-awareness:

- Check out a free personality test with 16Personalities.com or Truity.com, which base their tools off of the Myers Briggs personality test and which is a great place to start. This is not to put you further into a box, but instead to do some self-discovery about your personality. It's a good thing to actually take these at different intervals in career stage and age. We will dive deeper into personality tests in the next section.
- Keep a journal. This is a powerful tool for learning about yourself. Spend fifteen minutes each evening recording your life. List the meaningful things that happened that day. Include the challenges and what you think caused them.

Ask yourself:

- What did I do well?
- When did I not feel my authentic self?
- What beliefs were at the root of that situation?
- Are they true? Challenge the beliefs with truth statements over and over. This means to ask yourself, is this true? When has

this been true in the past? When has the opposite of this belief been true?

- What changes do I want to make? How will I make those changes?

Notice I did not focus on "achievement" as being a part of sense of self. Some folks tie this in, but I feel that is where some complications can happen, especially in the workplace.

Personality Tests: Use With Caution

I love personality tests! It's crazy I didn't take my first one until I was almost forty years old. I've taken many of the most popular tests including DISC (DI), Myers-Briggs, (ISTP) plus 16Personalities (INFJ-A), Predictive Index (Maverick), and Enneagram Personality Assessment (8). Some are a bit more focused on preferences over just personality. They typically offer great insight and honest validation for who you think you are. I've found the Enneagram to be the most helpful to me personally and in how I work with limiting beliefs in the challenge side of the work.

Using personality tests with teams in the past, I've figured out better ways to engage with others by understanding their personalities and not just what I assume about them. I also recognize when one of my qualities comes up that indicates I should stop being so assertive and be more collaborative. Being flexible in our engagements in managing people can really come into play here. One of my most commonly spoken phrases to my team over the past few years is, "We use psychology in business every day." It's about people. In reality, personality is not the truth of who you are, it's just the conditioned stuff. It's important to note that this means our true self or authentic self is not just based on the results of a personality test.

I've taken the DISC two times with very detailed reports on the outcome, so I want to make a point about environment, situation, and even personal state at the time of taking these tests. Here is a quick key to decode the DISC: D stands for Dominance, I is Influence, S is Steadiness, and C is Compliance. I like to think of the states the DISC measures as work (adaptive) and home (natural), but you can apply this approach to any environment (i.e., community, family, etc.). In 2014, I felt very comfortable in my job and driving goals like I was using a formula. My personal life was pretty balanced, so my "natural" and "adaptive" states were almost equal for each category in the results. I was prominently a DI. However, my S was much higher than it was the second time I took it in 2018 (four years later). Now remarried with five kiddos in our blended family and post-acquisition/integration of another company, my natural (home) state was a higher D then my adaptive (work) state, but my S state was much lower in both because I was freaking "busy," was dealing with a lot of unknowns and pressure with work, and trying to keep up with community commitments. What's interesting is that environment played a big role in why I shifted over those four years.

Unfortunately, many companies use personality tests to "filter" out candidates that don't fit their formula as a "fit" for them. Also, those done while on the job can actually be used against the employee. I've seen them used to look for flaws, instead of as a tool to see how teams can strengthen and leverage the different attributes of team members. The tests can be a scapegoat instead of a great learning tool to see where you are at that time and in the environment you are in. There is such a significant impact on the results based on the environment.

I'll share an observation over the past eight years of conducting the DISC assessment with Exploratory Lab Boot Camp students (college) and what I saw with two different team assessments over that four-year period I mentioned above. This is across almost two hundred students who have participated in one of the past ten boot camps. This has been one of their favorite parts of the boot camp. We have a wonderful soul, Jo Anne Myers of Sunstone International, LLC, deliver and coach them on how to utilize the information individually and as a team. The majority of students who took the DISC assessment scored pretty equally between natural and adaptive states across the board. Here is my quick reaction: "Wow, they can be their natural authentic self in their school environment."

When we conducted the DISC with my leadership team in 2014 and 2018, we found those who had been in the professional job and/or company between 15–25+ years (basically aged 39–55) had similar results. My quick reaction: "Great, they don't really care what others think and are confident in being their authentic self." Now here is what happened when we looked at the talented leaders in the professional job and/or company between 5–15 years (basically aged 28–38); they had a much higher DI in their adaptive (work) state then in their natural (home) state. Here is my quick reaction: "Wow, they are trying to prove themselves, second-guessing and over-analyzing to ensure they don't make mistakes." Dang. No wonder so many in their thirties decide they are not happy in their job or boss and leave. In reality, they do not feel they can show up authentically. Now I do realize there is a lot of pressure during those years in careers where we are trying to advance and are pushing ourselves to make more money. This could also cause the adaptive state to result higher.

Could this be a wake-up call to address what may be causing people unhappiness in their job, instead of using it against them in development plans or keeping them in a box until they quit? We hire people because we feel they will bring value to our team and business, we hire them for who we believe they are. Then when they adapt to an environment fueled by fear and competition, they change. When they change and can no longer show up as themselves, they become unhappy. When they become unhappy, they attach to a reason they are unhappy and, more often than not, it's not the real reason.

Make the Shift

Individuals: if you haven't taken a personality test before, I suggest doing it in a fun way. Try 16Personalities (which offers a real and great perspective and it's free) or an Enneagram assessment. Here's what to do with it.

1. Look for things where you say, "Yep, that's me." That's always fun.

2. Be open to the things that may offer guidance on how to better engage with others.

3. Identify anything that comes up that maybe gives guidance to something you felt was missing. Do something about it. This could be that you are a humanitarian, yet you are not involved in a "cause," or that you do/don't take constructive feedback well. Recognize this as an opportunity. For me as an 8 Enneagram, I have the opportunity to soften in my communication and to recognize that, to me, money is power and a way I can be controlled by others. Whoa. Yep, I'm working on that one.

4. Look for ways to align better on communication, preferences, and decisions, if you do this with your team or family. We may each be different, but we come together as one puzzle.

5. Have a Human Design assessment done instead of a personality test. This is such a hard-core, get-to-the-point guide on how to get things done, and your strategy and decision style. I'm a Manifesting Generator 2/4 who works from my inner authority of Emotional-Solar Plexus. It has been one of the MOST refreshing and specific tools I've used. Understanding my Strategy To Respond has reduced so much frustration for me. I've always thought I need to be an innovator and create from nothing. Nope. How I work best is to respond to what lights me up and is needed, and to get out of my head in that response creation. Check it out.

Make the Shift

Companies: if you want to use personality tests that's great, but really understand how the results are being used, and consult an expert on how to leverage this as a positive tool for growing teams and not limiting individuals.

27

WHAT DO YOU PUT OUT INTO THE WORLD?

Daring to set boundaries, is about having the courage to love ourselves
even when we risk disappointing others.
——Brené Brown

Perception Is Projection

What happens with all of that information (upwards of eleven million bits per second) coming to us, when we can only absorb 134 bits per second? It gets housed in our subconscious mind. We each take and either delete, distort, or generalize the information we do take in differently in order to make sense of it. Typically, what we absorb ends up becoming a belief. The subconscious mind's job is to protect us, keep our bodies going, and it has an ingrained fight, flight, or freeze mechanism to do so. Our ability to process information shapes our view of the world and how we view each other.

I've used this statement with my children and self when we come across someone who says something negative, mean, or hurtful to us. "What they are saying is how/what they feel about themselves. Don't take it personally, and show them compassion." Many times when you take a moment to just sit with what someone is actually saying, you realize this is out of left field, it's something they can't process, and is probably how they feel about themselves. Little did I know, this is actually a real thing discovered in the psychology and NLP (neuro-linguistic programming) worlds of research. It's called projection.

According to *Psychology Today*, projection is the process of displacing one's feelings onto a different person, animal, or object. The term is most commonly used to describe defensive projection—attributing one's own unacceptable urges to another. For example, if someone continuously bullies and ridicules a peer about his insecurities, the *bully* might be projecting his own struggle with *self-esteem* onto the other person. [17]

Sigmund Freud first reported on projection in an 1895 letter, in which he described a patient who tried to avoid confronting her feelings of *shame* by instead imagining that her neighbors were gossiping about her. More recent research has challenged Freud's hypothesis that people project to defend their egos. According to *Psychology Today*, "Projecting a threatening trait onto others may be a by-product of the mechanism that defends the ego, rather than a part of the defense itself. Trying to suppress a thought pushes it to the mental foreground, *psychologists have argued,* and turns it into a chronically accessible filter through which one views the world." [18]

One of the prime directives of the unconscious mind is that it takes everything personally. This is the basis of perception is projection. Perception is projection presupposes that we can only *perceive* what is already in our consciousness. [19] This comes from Carl Jung, who was a

---

[17] *Psychology Today.* blogs on:
Projection, https://www.psychologytoday.com/us/basics/projection -
Bullying, https://www.psychologytoday.com/us/basics/bullying -
Self-Esteem, https://www.psychologytoday.com/us/basics/self-esteem -
Embarrassment, https://www.psychologytoday.com/us/basics/embarrassment -
[18] L. S. Newman, K. J. Duff, K. J., R. F. Baumeister, "A new look at defensive projection: Thought suppression, accessibility, and biased person perception." *Journal of Personality and Social Psychology,* 72(5), 980–1001. 1997 - https://psycnet.apa.org/doi/10.1037/0022-3514.72.5.980
[19] Wayne Farrell, "Perception is Projection." - *CoachingwithNLP.com, (1997)* https://www.coachingwithnlp.co/perception-is-projection

Swiss psychologist and one of the three fathers of psychology, along with Freud and Alfred Adler. He said what we *perceive* is who we are. What we perceive outside ourselves is who we are. That means we can't perceive anything outside of ourselves that is not us. So whatever you perceive in someone else or something else is your projection. Projection explains how people can feel certain they know what another person is like and what they think, then interact with the other person based on those assumptions. Carl Jung and Marie-Louise von Franz argued that projection is also used to protect against the fear of the unknown, sometimes negatively impacting the projector. Within their framework, people project archetypal ideas onto things they don't understand as part of a natural response to the desire for a more predictable and clearly-patterned world.

What does authenticity mean when we don't "have control" over our subconscious mind? The good news is we actually do have the ability to leverage our subconscious mind to determine truth around situations, emotions, feelings, information, etc. This allows for us to identify when we are projecting and instead acknowledge why (emotions, feelings) we are projecting this to deal with it. Or when others are projecting onto us, we can acknowledge what they say, but not accept it as our truth. When we project onto others, we are typically working from the ego, which is not our authentic self. It's a part of our self, but typically conditioned and not fully authentic.

If someone has an unusually strong reaction to something you say, or there doesn't seem to be a reasonable explanation for their reaction, they might be projecting their insecurities onto you. Taking a step back to determine that their response doesn't align with your actions, may be a signal of projection. A parent who did not have a successful career may project onto their child that they won't either. A boss who is not happy with their current role and feels trapped may project onto their team member that they too will not have opportunities to be promoted. The cycle creates limiting beliefs if the person receiving the projection accepts it as truth.

One example of projecting in the workplace is if you've had a major disagreement with a colleague and are still feeling upset about it, you may perceive their subsequent behavior as hostile toward you, when others maintain that it is not. Another example is when you are irritated by the behavior of a colleague, but it's really yourself you're irritated with. I've done this when I wasn't meeting my expectations and then projected those high expectations on another. Projection can happen with positive traits we struggle to acknowledge as well. Think about a time when you were part of a team and played a key role on a successful project, but you blew off compliments and appreciation by a stakeholder. Or maybe you show you are pleased with someone else, yet it's really yourself you're pleased with.

We should ask ourselves, "What is it in me that I need to deal with so that I can stop having this negative experience?" How can we deal with what we are projecting, so that we don't have a major negative reaction to it? We could say, "If I have negative emotions about someone, I can be sure that it is a projection." Whether I have positive emotions or negative emotions, they are incorporated inside of me. Because everything is a projection. When your interaction has become "stuck" in bad feelings, polarized points of view, or a complete lack of empathy, projection comes out. When your fears or insecurities are provoked, it's natural to occasionally begin projecting.

Make the Shift

Here is how to recognize when you are projecting. Similar to working with our inner critic, limiting beliefs, and other reactions, first step away from the conflict to reduce your defensiveness and reach your rational mind. Follow these steps to explore whether and why you may have been projecting.

1. Describe the conflict in objective terms.
2. Describe the actions that you took and the assumptions you made.
3. Describe in order the actions the other person took and the assumptions they made.

Protective Boundaries

I've mentioned boundaries in previous chapters and the need to set healthy boundaries. This can be challenging for many of us, because either we are always taking care of everyone else or being the problem-solver or the overachiever, and we don't want to disappoint others. It's a good thing to have healthy boundaries in the workplace as well. What I've seen instead is people being taken advantage of, overwhelmed, not speaking truth, and having what I call protective boundaries. Unhealthy boundaries create barriers across organizations and within teams including lack of collaboration and unhealthy competition, and restrict expansion and innovation.

We definitely feel the need to protect our energy, space, team, decisions, actions, responsibilities, and value. Sometimes, though, we become very protective and set boundaries that can actually limit us and others around us. For instance, when we become *territorial* about our team, responsibilities, or space, we can actually make decisions that are not the best for our team, selves, or business. We limit ourselves from seeing the big picture, supporting the overall cause, and allowing for growth. "That's my job" is a very prominent defense mechanism heard in the workplace that is used to keep others from encroaching in our territory. "That's my team" or "those are my customers" is another defense mechanism used in territory protection. "My team is the best to do that task" is used to ensure their team stays in place and holds on to their value. Hierarchical structures have created a very specific role or person expectation along with a decision tree that will be very limiting if not restructured appropriately during transformations.

Protecting our energy is a big deal in the workplace and can impact how we show up in an authentic way. If we feel that certain people suck the life out of us, we may avoid them or email versus meeting/calling them. There are also tasks that can drain our energy that keep us imprisoned to the energy drain. Is the task even necessary? Are there different ways to do the task? Is there a different day or longer time to get it done to avoid the drain? Can it be automated?

Our personal lives become very protected as well, since we don't want the fact we are married, have children, or have caregiver responsibilities for family members to hold us back from opportunities or from keeping our job. We feel we have to apologize when we need to leave early to pick up a sick child from school or daycare or have to take a few hours to go to a doctor's appointment to take care of ourselves. Taking care of our family and ourselves is a priority, and we don't need to justify anything to anyone. In order to bring down the protective boundaries around our personal situations, there needs to be trust, freedom, and respect by managers and companies to support colleagues.

Decisions, actions, and our value become protected as we hold onto our significance by proving that we made the best decision/action. We can become blinded by other options and again struggle with zooming out to the big picture. Instead of shutting others out while setting up protective boundaries, there is a better way to shift in the workplace.

Not a boundary: "No way am I working with that team, they have their own priorities."

A boundary: "Once we align on goals, I would like to partner with that team."

Not a boundary: "I'm not a superhero; I can't do everything. What don't you understand?"

A boundary: "Going forward, I won't be able to submit this report to you by Thursday. I can do it by Friday at five p.m."

Not a boundary: "You're making decisions based on your personal agenda, and that's not fair."

A boundary: "I feel very hurt when you don't consider me in making decisions. Going forward, I will need to be included in making them."

There are many types of boundaries we can set in a healthy way including:

- Emotional boundaries where we can stand in "I'm not comfortable talking about ... ,"
- Time boundaries where we can stand in "I can't help you today, but I have time on Wednesday,"
- Topic boundaries where we can stand in "If there will be gossip, I'm not coming," and
- Physical boundaries where we can stand in "I check my email the first two hours when I get into the office. I will respond to you then."

These are great responses to set healthy boundaries and expectations in a clear way.

Healthy boundaries at work can also sound like this:

- "I'm honored that you would ask me to help, but I'm unable to add anything else with my workload."
- "I can't lower my price, and I hope that you find someone within your budget."
- "I know I'm working from home, but I'm still maintaining normal business hours."
- "I can't offer my services for free."

- "I need help with my workload, because I can't manage everything on my plate."
- "I'm not able to chat right now; I need to stay focused on my current assignment."
- "I'd rather talk by phone instead of emailing about this topic."

Protective boundaries may not be healthy boundaries, and really addressing how you set up boundaries in the workplace can not only help you with energy, space, and time, but help your team, culture, and business have more flow, happiness, authenticity, and collaboration.

Setting time aside for you, tasks, learning, team members, etc. is also setting boundaries (to support your priorities). The most important things to consider in the workplace are around what you value (well-being, energy, clarity, growth, honesty). You need to say no when it's not a true yes. Guard your personal time, test your limits and be real with yourself and others. Honor your needs and values by staying true when there is external pressure. Dedicate time for yourself, take action even when you're afraid, and address and adjust boundaries as needed.

Make the Shift

Six tips to set healthy boundaries:

1. Be clear about what you want. Write your purpose in pen and your path in pencil.
2. Don't keep anyone guessing with ambiguousness or a lack of communication. Communicate clear expectations.
3. Be direct and don't apologize for your needs. I finally stopped providing a reason or apology when I couldn't attend a meeting or make a work event. This is a habit to get rid of—it's nobody's business why you can't do something.
4. Expect resistance and don't let it throw you off or keep you from staying firm on boundaries.

5. Remember that setting boundaries is an ongoing process. Be aware, assess, and set.
6. Set boundaries for your own well-being, not to control others.

28

WHAT DO YOU HOLD DEAR?

Authenticity and self-trust are about 1) knowing and owning who you really are and 2) removing everything that you are not and liberating your true self.
——Violetta Pleshakova

What Are Your Personal Stories?

Your personal stories have been drafted over your entire lifetime. They also include past generation stories as well. Our stories are based on how we perceived them, yet others may have a different point of view or remembrance. Many stories come and go and don't necessarily cause us challenges in the future, but many can absolutely impact our decisions, reactions, and suffering. Many are based on how you were raised. It's your narrative you learned from parents, your society and culture and can be generationally based.

Your stories formed from what your parents taught you, but you mostly learned by observing their behavior, their interactions, and their emotions when anything challenging or opportunistic was in the air. Your personal story helps to shape your current mindset. You have three very personal core relationships that create many of your stories: your relationship with money, food, and yourself.

Think back to your earliest or most prevalent memories. What was the feeling about money like in the home where you grew up? What was the feeling like about spending money? Saving money? Giving money away? What was your earliest money memory? What was the message from your mother? Father? (I'm not referring to "how-tos," but rather actual message/attitude about money.) Do you remember your parents talking about (or fighting about) money? Did your parents buy you anything you wanted? Did you have to sell things in your house to avoid something terrible from happening? Did you get an allowance, or did you have to earn it by doing chores? Did a parent shop and then hide their purchases? Did your parents talk about how much things cost or how much money they earned? Did you feel that you had "as much" as your friends? What did you do with money you received when you were young (save/spend)? How have your answers about money shaped your story?

Now think back to your earliest or most prevalent memories about food. Did you go without food? Was there always food available? Did you use food to make you feel better? Was food thought of as a tool? Did you have sit-down dinners with your family? Did you eat on the run? Was food wasted? Was food healthy? Were there negative comments around food and eating? Was the word diet used frequently in your house growing up? What was your mother's message around food? Father's message? Did you grow your own food? Was there a scarcity mindset around food? How have your answers about food shaped your story?

Now think back to your earliest or most prevalent memories about yourself. Did you have issues with your body? Were you in a safe environment—or not? Were you careful not to get hurt or be reckless with your body? Did you trust yourself? Were you confident in your abilities? Were you supported? Did you look within to find strength or outside of yourself? Did you trust your intuition? Did you have an imaginary friend? Did others criticize you? For what? Were you bullied by classmates or family members? Were you kind to yourself, or did you beat yourself up regularly? Did you talk nicely to yourself or did your "Fred" chime in? How have your answers about yourself shaped your story?

Now think back to your earliest or most prevalent memories about work ethic. Did your parents have a certain work ethic growing up? Was it expected of you? Did you get to see your parents work or understand what they did for work? Were you supported in activities you wished to participate in or criticized that you weren't good enough? Did you have freedom to explore as a child? Were you included in chores, tasks, or creating around the house (dinner, cleaning, building, fixing, etc.)? Were you supported in school? Were grades important in your household, and to you? Was trying your best expected? How have your answers about work ethic shaped your story?

Now think back to your earliest or most prevalent memories about trust. Did you trust your parents and family members? Did you trust teachers, neighbors, and authority figures? What was the earliest memory of someone breaking your trust? What impact did this have on your childhood? Did your parents or caregivers trust each other? Did they trust others like neighbors, institutions, bosses, or coworkers? Were they vocal about their own trust issues that you overheard? How have your answers about trust shaped your story?

Make the Shift

Write your personal story, or stories.

1. Take out a piece of paper and write out your personal story. You can tap into other areas similar to above and include in your story.
2. Look back over your story and find those areas that are impacting your current situation in life and career.
3. Challenge their truth and rewrite your story.

What Are You Thankful For?

Being thankful throughout our day for what we have, can do, and can be is a great way to be in your authentic self. I started a gratitude practice to help me get out of the autopilot mode and into a thankful way of being. Life is an initiation full of trials and tribulations, most of which we probably signed up for to help elevate ourselves in this life. When we focus on the challenges only and don't see the lesson or benefit that may come later, we live in a perpetual motion of fear and worry. Living in gratitude helps to break the cycle.

Why a gratitude practice? In our busy everyday life routines, we can become a bit robotic. Taking a few moments throughout the day to really feel and show gratitude for what and who we have in our lives brings joy and grounding and opens up positive things in life. A start is setting aside time in a "ritual," whether morning or evening.

How to feel gratitude. Make this your own. I like to visualize and feel gratitude in my heart space for people/things/events/situations. I practice this in the morning as a structured ritual and then throughout the day as little moments of help, kindness, and appreciation. Taking a second to acknowledge, feel, and be thankful evolves a gratitude practice into living a thankful life. You can keep a gratitude journal—do what works for you.

Living a Thankful Life. As the awareness of your day opens up, you become more mindful. These moments of feeling gratitude shifts to being thankful for all of life, including the "negative." I view a gratitude practice as the foundation for shifting to living a thankful life.

What are you thankful for?

29

LET'S DEEP DIVE

A lot of the conflict you have in your life exists simply because you're not living in alignment; you're not being true to yourself.
——Steve Maraboli, *Unapologetically You: Reflections of Life and the Human Experience*

What Are Your Needs and Wants?

Needs are important to differentiate from wants. This helps as you set budgets, make investments, go for promotions or new jobs, and determine spending. Needs are those things that we require in order to survive and include food, water, shelter, clothing (basics/uniform), healthcare and/or therapy, medication, and human connection. Defining our needs, including relationships, is really important to ensure we protect both money and the time allocated to our needs. Planning and decisions become much easier. We can then stay true to our basic needs.

Wants are quite a bit more expansive. It includes what we wish or desire to procure like homes, dining out, entertainment, new clothing, travel, TV or music streaming accounts, monthly subscriptions, and memberships. Wants and desires become motivation as well as needs when it comes to seeking increased income, starting a business, or other passive income. Wants and desires also begin to form our dream plans.

Even the smallest beliefs can have the most profound impact on your mindset and openness to opportunities, or they can hold you back. This is where self-sabotage comes into play. If you've listened to my solo episode (#2) on Shifting Inside Out podcast on self-sabotage, you'll understand where I'm going with this. If not, bear with me. The work you did in part 1 to shift your limitations and mindset can help to open up your ability to dream, plan, and take action instead of sabotaging any area.

Determining what your true desires are is super-critical to ensure you don't (subconsciously) sabotage them. Then shift your mindset by tackling limiting beliefs to achieving your dreams. Creating goals with timelines gives purpose to "how" you will get to your dreams. It doesn't end there. Realizing your dreams means staying connected to them, tracking results and adjusting as you go.

As you determine your wants and desires, think about what you really want and not just what you wanted last year or in the past, or what you think you can have based on your current situation. This creates limitations on what you could actually have, and what I've found is it won't happen if you don't truly want it!

Everyone has dreams. Some are much larger and more complex than others, but they all have value. The dreams that you have are there for a reason: to be realized as a part of fulfilling your life purpose. Many people give up on their dreams because they don't see them coming to pass when planned. Have patience! Although your dream may not have come to pass yet, it can still be realized.

In addition to physically working toward your dreams, mental preparation is important. That means you need to keep visualizing and dreaming. Hold on to what you believe in and what you want to see happen in your life. Use the power of positive thinking in order to see your dream coming to fruition. Being specific about what you want to achieve is really important in order to take action. Dream every day using different tools to keep the dream alive.

One of the best visualization techniques I've found to really set in your desires and bring to life the future you of your desires is to focus on how you feel, look, your energy (happiness), and health. You can find the Meet Your Future Self-guided journey recording in your bonuses that come with this book at www.angiemccourt.com/loveyourgifts. You may include your work environment, hobbies, a new business, or even writing and publishing a book. Where you live and details of your home and community are great to include. Other important details to include are your ideal day, morning routine, "work day," family/friends, cooking, gardening, exercise, or other important future-self items. Go all in and visualize what you truly want!

I love this exercise as it is one of the most motivating for each area of your life you wish to focus on. It's important to write out your future self and visualize it as if it's in the present. Use the guided visualization journey recording until the picture and feelings of your future self become part of your everyday vision. This will help you stick to your plan: financial, health, self-care, time and energy spend, career, education, and anything else you desire and want. You can add more details each time you listen. One key is to use your senses. Feel, smell, see, hear, and taste your future.

Make the Shift

Define your wants and desires. Take a piece of paper or journal and write down what it is you truly need and want/desire.

Make the Shift

Meet your future self.

1. Listen to the guided journey recording.

Picture what you want and write out your story as if it is your current life and self. Your future self is a great story. Bringing it to the present tense brings a reality to it that helps you to set goals, motivate to achieve them, and improve your current state, allowing flow and abundance into your life.

What Are Your Values?

Core values are your lighthouse, illuminating the pathway toward living a meaningful life filled with passion and purpose. Core values are foundational to building a sense of purpose and direction. You may appear to be successful, but still feel lost. Defining what success means to you reduces cycles of chasing empty accomplishments. If you don't understand your values, you may violate them without realizing it. This can lead to feelings of guilt and shame, without knowing why. What is really interesting is how your core values can change based on where you are in your life.

When you are a young parent, your core values center more around your family, and as your family grows and your career expands, your core values shift. They can shift to more personal growth, spirituality, contribution, giving, and freedom. We will do a deep-dive exercise in a moment, but I suggest evaluating your core values every year to ensure you stay aligned with them. Once you decide your top five core values, keep them in front of you. Align priorities and actions to them to build the habits in alignment with decision-making and behaviors.

Researchers confirm that when people have a clear set of core values:

- Their life decisions around pursuing passions, career goals, long-term life goals, and relationships are easier and more aligned.
- They are less likely to engage in negative thought patterns, especially in difficult life situations.
- They have a higher physical pain tolerance, greater self-discipline and focus, and stronger social connections.[20]

---

[20] Anna Mikulak, "The Heart of the Matter," Association for Psychological Science, July 29, 2016, https://www.psychologicalscience.org/observe/the-heart-of-the-matter

29 LET'S DEEP DIVE

When it comes to core values, there's no "one size fits all" approach. Everyone is different. Here are just some ideas included in this list of core values to review.

Family	Personal Growth	Friendship
Freedom	Learning	Courage
Security	Flow	Balance
Loyalty	Honesty	Compassion
Intelligence	Adventure	Fitness
Connection	Kindness	Professionalism
Creativity	Teamwork	Relationship
Humanity	Career	Knowledge
Success	Communication	Patience
Respect	Learning	Change
Invention	Excellence	Prosperity
Generosity	Innovation	Wellness
Integrity	Quality	Finances
Love	Commonality	Gratitude
Openness	Contributing	Grace
Religion	Spiritualism	Endurance
Order	Strength	Facilitation
Advancement	Entertainment	Effectiveness
Respect	Wealth	Fun
Joy/Play	Speed	Fame
Forgiveness	Power	Justice
Working Smarter	Affection	Appreciation
Diligence	Cooperation	Willingness
Excitement	Love of Career	Trusting Your Gut
Change	Relationship	Patience
Goodness	Encouragement	Forgiveness

Involvement	Pride in Work	Self-Respect
Faith	Clarity	Abundance
Wisdom	Fun-Loving	Reciprocity
Beauty	Charisma	Enjoyment
Caring	Humor	Entrepreneurial
Contentment	Leadership	Happiness
Peace	Renewal	Harmony
Being True	Home	

For example, if you chose the core value of freedom, you value the power or right to act, speak, or think as one wants without restraint and the freedom to work, live, and spend your time the way you choose.

Here are examples of actions you could take to align more fully with freedom as a core value in your life:

- Express yourself freely and openly.
- Build a life in which you can create your own schedule, travel, location, etc.
- Nurture relationships with friends and family who give you the freedom to be yourself.
- Become your own boss or share your expectations of flexibility in your workday.
- Include enough free time in your schedule to do what you enjoy.

Make the Shift

Complete the steps below to see where these values show up in your life:

1. Pick the top ten core values from the list above or add your own.

2. Narrow it down to your top five. What truly resonates with you at this time in your life?

3. Define the value for each one. What does it mean to you?

4. Identify the actions and activities that reflect each of these values.

5. Find what else you could do to further align yourself with each of these values.

6. Determine if you could do more to include these values in your daily life.

What Are Your Beliefs?

It's interesting to pay attention to all of the thoughts that come into our minds daily. They are based on what we see, hear, and feel, and on our past experiences. We analyze, generalize, delete, or just discard them. The ones we hold onto have a potent power over us. They become housed in our subconscious mind and are pulled out when we need them. Your beliefs are just thoughts and your thoughts can be changed. We have hit on limiting beliefs and their impact on our authenticity throughout this book, so now we are going to do some work to discover your core beliefs.

Our belief system is underlying pretty much everything we do, say, and think. It's there to guide us and we trust in it. Core beliefs affect our inner monologue. They shift over the years as new experiences bring a different perspective or as we debunk the belief with truth. We can also shift them. Instead of allowing past experience or outside influences like media, pop culture, or social environment to shape your life, you can be true to yourself and solidify your own core beliefs. I'd like to focus on building the positive core beliefs you may align to instead of focusing on limiting beliefs.

Here are some examples of personal core beliefs:

1. *I choose to trust myself.* I am the first person I trust. I live with integrity and by my core values. Choice is the most powerful tool I have.

2. *I choose to believe that my life is meaningful.* Every day I show kindness, gratitude, and intention. I give my life meaning.

3. *Everything will turn out all right.* It always turns out just fine in the end. I look forward to the full story unveiling itself.

4. *Every day is the most important day of my life.* I live each day with purpose. I put my best foot forward. I appreciate the opportunities this day brings.

5. *Everyone I meet has a purpose or a message for me.* We are all connected and when I meet someone, I listen. I ask them questions. I seek the message. I enjoy the connection.

6. *Life is an initiation, not a problem to be fixed.* This life is just the beginning of something more. I learn from my lessens, when presented. Of course, I struggle; I'm a spiritual being living in human form.

7. *I choose to leave a legacy having done my best and having given everything.* Every day I put my heart and energy into being purposeful. I live in an aligned way. This empowers others to do the same. I touch so many. They love and embrace themselves.

8. *No one really cares about me as much as I think. This is incredibly liberating.* Thank goodness I no longer hold tight to others' opinions of me. I do appreciate their feedback, but I don't dwell on what I assume they think. Not everyone is for me. I can't control what others think of me.

9. *It's always OK to say no, and it's always OK to ask for help.* Saying no is my superpower. I do it with ease and grace. I am not afraid to ask for help. I know when I need help. I don't know everything, so I ask others for help.

10. *By taking care of myself first, I can better care for the world.* I listen to my body. I set healthy boundaries for myself. I recharge myself so I can recharge others.

11. *When my heart is open, love flows in.* I live each day with an open heart. This has reduced my stress. When a tough situation comes up, I lead with love. I open my heart to others.

These are some examples of core beliefs that great leaders practice daily:

1. *I lead by example in as many areas as possible.* Through leading by example, others see that I'm committed too. I see others' loyalty increase.

2. *I intentionally balance vision and execution. I maintain focus and pay attention to my intentions.* I create alignment to vision and inspire others to help me carry out the vision. My focus keeps others engaged and committed.

3. *My actions and words deliver inspiration. Optimism is my superpower.* My inspired actions motivate others to achieve their goals. I filter out the static and keep the message aligned. My optimism is contagious.

4. *My intention is to always show respect, and I envelope humility.* I listen closely to others' ideas. I begin with an open mind. I look for common ground and get out of my comfort zone. I seek understanding and ask questions. I show respect through my actions. I keep my emotions in check.

5. *I exhibit confidence in how I lead and make decisions.* My confidence increases daily as I take courageous action. I may not always be fully confident, but when I believe in something, I influence others. My decisions are the best I can make at that time with the information and experiences I have.

6. *I accept accountability for my actions, decisions, and for the words I use.* I will make the best decisions I can. I will own

alternative solutions and the results of those decisions, actions, and words. I will point the finger at myself before anyone else.

7. *I am committed to being courageous. I take risks and learn from my mistakes.* My courage grows daily. I'm excited to challenge myself to be courageous. I speak up when there is an idea I believe in. I speak up when something needs to be challenged. I push the envelope forward.

8. *I show appreciation for my team, coworkers, customers, opportunities, and challenges.* There is nothing I can do without the people around me. I appreciate them in many ways, but always be sure to show them. Silent appreciation is like no appreciation. I know others light up when I show them appreciation. I look at challenges as an opportunity to grow and make things better.

9. *My investment in others makes my work more meaningful.* One of my biggest joys in my day is taking time to invest in others. I make time for them. I look for ways to help them increase their skills. I inspire them to reach higher.

10. When you make the time to invest in others, they will return great value. When you invest in your people, you are investing in the future.

11. *I lead with integrity. I believe in and practice fairness every day.* My integrity is at my core. I live my integrity every day. I treat others in a fair way and don't show favoritism, even if it's easy to do so. I don't exclude others.

12. *Communication is an important tool I embrace.* I communicate fully. I speak and I listen. I use communication to make connections with my team to our vision and goals. I am strategic in my messages so they are clear and timely. I don't hide information.

13. *I embody honesty and honor trust.* I know my integrity requires me to be true and honest. I am transparent. I trust others before they need to "earn" it. I share my intentions and don't hide behind a hidden agenda.

Make the Shift

Trying something new is part of the initiation of life.

1. Find one personal and one leadership belief you'd most like to take on.

2. Relax your assumptions and experiment with trying it on for thirty days to see if it's true for you or not. If you don't connect with it, at least you've learned something about yourself.

30

CHECK ON YOUR MINDSET

Fear makes us defensive when we live in the fixed mindset, but it makes us adaptive in the growth mindset.

——Dr. Carole Dweck, *Mindset, The New Psychology of Success*

Fixed Versus Growth Mindset

There is an interesting approach to mindset that has been identified and categorized by Dr. Carole Dweck's research and adopted in corporate environments. One of the biggest supporters of this concept is Microsoft. For many years they have shared programs with their colleagues around fixed versus growth mindset. I personally feel that there are things that keep us in a certain mindset once we enter the workplace influenced by expectations and fear. As we dive into fixed and growth mindsets, I'll call out some specific things that do limit us in trying to shift to a growth mindset within the workplace. I also view these as opportunities you can recognize that may be limiting your ability to be your authentic mindset and for companies to make changes.

First, let's define a fixed mindset using Dr. Carole Dweck's work. A fixed mindset can come across as the knower (with a fixed intelligence) who doesn't want feedback, and they do not like to veer off track. They limit themselves from taking risks because they cannot fail. This means they avoid challenges, give up easily (obstacles), and see failure as fruitless or worse (effort) and talent as innate, so effort and practice is not important. They ignore useful negative feedback (criticism) and can feel threatened by the success of others. As a result, they may plateau and achieve less than their full potential. Being in a fixed mindset can also emit behaviors like stubbornness, hiding flaws and mistakes, and being unmotivated to achieve goals. Feelings like shame, jealousy, and contentment can underly their mindset.

A growth mindset believes intelligence and talents can be improved, so they are learners and appreciate regular feedback, reflection, and iteration as an opportunity to grow. They celebrate risks and failures as essential to mastery. They embrace flaws and mistakes as opportunities for growth and feel empowered to reach goals. They view other people's success as a source of inspiration.

Why wouldn't you want a growth mindset? Of course, the push to shift our fixed mindset to one of a growth mindset is a natural shift happening through engagement alone. It's almost like we are giving permission to each other to make the shift to a more growth mindset view and approach. It's becoming part of our authentic self. Here is where the challenge comes in the workplace: structure, old ways of doing things, and keeping us in the box. I'll dive into just three areas that are top of mind that definitely go against our shift to a growth mindset.

Fear of failure in the workplace is an underlying constraint that holds us in a fixed mindset. There is a cultural shift that needs to happen in this case. This can happen from top down or grass roots with support from the top leaders through leading by example, having processes in place that don't shame failure, and encouragement to shift a project or transaction to success through empowerment and enablement. Encourage experimentation without even using words like "failure."

There are too many policies in the workplace that create a black and white environment. These limit decision-making and creative problem-solving and totally take the "lead" out of leader. It has basically created a crutch, and the creativity of being in business and managing people all comes down to what is written, based on some people's perspective who created the policies in the first place. As we have seen such a huge need for our AQ (adaptive quotient—I'll get into this in part 3) to evolve (yes, evolve and quickly), we haven't removed obstacles that are stagnant, outdated, set in place, or black and white policies. This becomes either a battle of frustration or creates complacency.

Status quo is such a dirty little phrase. It's one that deep down we want to challenge and change, but how do we do that if there is an ego tied to it (the person who created it to begin with), or it's so complex that to untangle it would be significant. I just had this conversation with my son, who started a new job. I said, "Make sure you ask questions, and don't just rely on the person training you, ask others." They learned their job from someone else and probably never challenged how to do the job. Expansion of our viewpoint is so important, and just because something has always been done a certain way, does not mean that is the best or most effective way to do it. When we look at how we shift from a fixed to a growth mindset in a culture where you "can't challenge status quo," or feel it's futile to do so because it seems nothing will change, people don't care enough to make the change, or someone will keep it from happening, it's pretty difficult to actually show up with your growth mindset.

Recognition for natural talents or intelligence encourages the push to a fixed mindset. Instead, recognize effort and the process one takes to accomplish a goal and focus on the strategies they came up with and/or the persistence to achieve. I remember one of my field sales folks took four years to land a customer. I loved her persistence and never-give-up attitude while always focusing on how she could better serve that customer. It's important to recognize resilience as well. In this age of much change, innovation, and "transformation," resilience is a valiant skill.

The last limit I'll dive into is around industry standard. This also forces you into the status quo box, whether it's around how the industry or your company views the "best" way to get something done. When we become robots performing around industry standard, it kills individuality. The real successes are not industry standard, they are innovation. We just live by the myths that you have to do things a certain way. Defy industry standards— challenge which things you are doing that are industry standard that don't serve you and keep you trapped in the box.

Of course, looking at authenticity means the true self, which at this time could mean having a fixed mindset. It's up to you to make a shift and try out some different ways of thinking and doing. Much work needs to be done around limiting beliefs, which can be how you are set in a fixed mindset. Why is our mindset so important to our progress? Being in a fixed mindset can keep you from exploring, responding, and engaging in expansive ways. It limits learning potential and can impact relationships. A growth mindset provides an opportunity to open up to different solutions, opportunities, and talents. I'm not saying let's all switch to a growth mindset, but let's make sure that, for those trying to use their authentic mindset in the workplace, the environment aligns with these new expectations.

Part 1 Make the Shift

Do you have a fixed or growth mindset? To find out, start by reading the following statements and decide which ones you agree with most:

1. You're born with a certain amount of intelligence, and it isn't something that can be changed.
2. No matter who you are, there isn't much you can do to improve your basic abilities and personality.
3. People are capable of changing who they are.
4. You can learn new things and improve your intelligence.

5. People either have particular talents, or they don't. You can't just acquire talent for things like music, writing, art, or athletics.

6. Studying, working hard, and practicing new skills are all ways to develop new talents and abilities.

If you tend to agree most with statements 1, 2, and 5, then you probably have a more fixed mindset. If you agree most with statements 3, and 4, 6, then you probably tend to have a growth mindset.

Part 2 Make the Shift

While people with a fixed mindset might not agree, Dweck suggests that people are capable of changing their mindsets. Here's how to unfix a fixed mindset.

1. Focus on the journey. An important factor when building a growth mindset is seeing the value in your journey. When you're fixated on the end result, you miss out on all the things you could be learning along the way.

2. Incorporate "yet." If you're struggling with a task, remind yourself that you just haven't mastered it "yet." Integrating this word into your vocabulary signals that, despite any struggles, you can overcome anything.

3. Pay attention to your words and thoughts. Replace negative thoughts with more positive ones to build a growth mindset.

4. Take on challenges. Making mistakes is one of the best ways to learn. So, instead of shying away from challenges, embrace them.

Cause and Effect

Take a moment today and listen to those around you: your family, co-workers, and neighbors. Are they living in "cause" or "effect"? You may be thinking, "OK, now what is she talking about?" So much of our conversational flow in daily life can indicate the mindset we have formed around how life is happening to us, not for us. Listen for things like, "I don't have time," "I'm late for work," "I'm waiting on so-and-so to finish this report," "I can't complete this project without resources," and "I just can't get promoted." Living in effect, which is reliant on something or someone, creates reasons and excuses as to why something is not happening in our lives.

The law of cause and effect is a universal law which specifically states that every effect has a specific and predictable cause. Every single action in the universe produces a reaction, no matter what. Every single item within the universe is relative, and nothing is separate. This means that everything that we currently have in our lives is an *effect* that is a result of a specific *cause*. These *causes* are the decisions we make and the actions we take on a daily basis. Whether our decisions seem small and rather insignificant, or whether they are significant and transformational in nature does not matter. Each and every decision we have made and action we have taken has set events into motion creating predictable and specific *effects* that we are now experiencing in our lives. In short, the law states that there are no accidents in this world, and that the *effects* we create in our lives are a direct result of *causes* that come from within ourselves. What you attract into your life is a direct result of the *causes* you brought forth into existence.

This basically means that achieving success in any field of endeavor is predictable and can be repeated if we are aware of what we are doing. Which essentially means that if you make the right decisions and take the right actions, you will undoubtedly achieve the success you envision for your life—whether you are directly aware of it or not. We are experiencing *life as we know it* because of the learned and conditioned psychological patterns we have preprogrammed into our minds over a lifetime of free choice. Moreover, this psychological programming is filtering our experience of reality in a very biased yet very predictable way—effectively creating and interpreting our existence in front of our eyes. Free choice means that we can *make a different choice* and choose to *unlearn* what we have learned and *learn* what it will take to trigger the *causes* that will create the *effects* we desire to experience within our lives.

Within our individual thoughts lie the origins of the *causes* we create in our reality. These *causes* create *effects* which we experience in our lives as manifested life circumstances. In fact, our thoughts do more than just that. They actually give meaning to our experience of reality, which is why each of us holds a different perspective of the world around us. Living in *effect* can impact authenticity as well, since we are not really owning the outcomes and path to achieving them. We then rely on reasons as to why not and think life is happening to us. In an authentic and empowered state, we are able to take the actions needed to shift to a cause state and live as if life is happening for us.

As we look back to many of the limitations addressed in previous chapters, we see how effect can take shape in the workplace, especially when we don't feel we can show up as our authentic self. Feeling the need to prove ourselves, compare and compete in unhealthy ways even with our identity as well as holding judgment, a fixed mindset, and unrealistic expectations can all play a role in living in effect. This shows up in the workplace as a survival mechanism, especially in fear-based cultures and environments lacking accountability. You may be familiar with the "throwing hands up in the air" (out of my control), finger-pointing, blame/shame, or "it's not my job" behaviors that occur when "things" happen in effect in a colleague's area of responsibility. It's healthy for each of us to make a shift from effect to cause, but we can also help those around us do the same through awareness and suggestion.

Making the shift from *effect* to *cause* can be life-changing. Making this change where you find repeat challenges in achieving goals or in relationships can help shift how those situations and people interact in your life. Focus on your words, actions, body, and thoughts to identify what may be holding you back.

Make the Shift

Here are some questions to ask yourself and action to take to get into shifting to *cause* in your daily and work life.

- How are my thoughts causing, creating, and maintaining my current life circumstances?
- How can I begin interpreting my world differently?
- How can I change my patterns of thinking?
- Take one action step toward your goal every single day. Even if it is a small one, you will inevitably move closer to your end goal. *It is not physically or scientifically possible for you to stay in the same place.*

31

YOUR PERSONAL POWER

Your personal power is not something that is going to reveal itself at some later date. Your power is a result of your decision to reveal it. You are powerful in whatever moment you choose to be.
——Marianne Williamson

Your Authentic Self

Authenticity unleashes your gifts. Authenticity is really the key to personal power as well. Authenticity allows you to build confidence and allows others to trust you. Authenticity allows for healthier relationships. It's aligned to your values, beliefs, personal stories, and boundaries. It unleashes your gifts! When you are not being your authentic self, you will suffer. Showing up in your authentic skin may not always be easy or simple, but it's what drives you and what keeps you connected to yourself. It brings a sense of grounded knowing and peace that you cannot find in external sources. It's what you brought here to this life with you.

Tony Robbins sets this question at the core. "Who did you have to be to feel loved or accepted as a child?" How does that inform who you have to be today? A good exercise to do right now is think about the areas of your life where you feel you cannot be your authentic self. Where does it sit the most, work, home, relationships, or community? Pick the one area you'd like to dig into first.

There are some key areas to focus on in order to feel your authentic self. Have compassion for yourself and others—positive words, actions, and feelings through nurturing. Vulnerability is a good thing! You are not expected to know everything. Vulnerability creates trust with others. Perfection is not a strength or weakness, it's an outcome of fear and feeling a lack of control. Releasing attachments to outcomes and perfection in getting there is important. Listen to your inner guidance, your intuition. We already know everything we need to know—trust it, and listen to it.

Learn to be assertive. I don't mean be an ass; find ways to own your message in a way it does not get lost. Live in a purposeful way, and don't get into the trap of seeking out your purpose in a backwards way. Life purpose is closely linked to authenticity, and living authentically displays your life purpose (hint hint).

Growing thick skin is fine as long as, at the end of the day, it's still your skin.

Many times situations and challenges form our growth, enable our confidence, and/or give us our voice. I like to call this our life initiation. These experiences "thicken our skin" and we either only want to survive, or we look at it as an opportunity to grow. The most important thing to keep in mind is to stay true to yourself. Keep YOUR skin.

Resourcefulness

Resourcefulness is defined by the *Oxford English Dictionary* as the ability to find quick and clever ways to overcome difficulties. I'll add and to achieve goals. When you are able to tap into your resourceful abilities, you unlock an entire side of you that can unleash your elevated gifts. You become more accountable for your own life, path, and decisions and find creative ways to achieve your goals or overcome an obstacle. There are many ways you can be resourceful, and I'm going to focus on the key areas in the workplace.

Understand your company's business model. The more you get into the "why" goals are set the way they are, how financial models and reporting is used to make decisions, and who the decision-makers are within the model, the more you will be able to get things done. You will be able to challenge what no longer aligns to agreed-upon goals and outcomes. You will be able to foresee the "red flags" before they become "red flags." You will be able to see the "big picture" to better understand how you contribute or can improve contribution. Get out of your comfort zone to increase your knowledge, confidence, and personal power.

Know your environment. Not just your team or physical location, but the entire environment. How can you navigate it to get things done? If you are in an environment highly-dependent on others to get your own job done, then building relationships, understanding their goals and struggles, as well as improving connection into their processes will be extremely helpful. I always looked at time getting to know people and their processes in other departments as an investment. That short amount of time up front saved me so much time down the road.

Building relationships with people also gives you priority. Even when someone's process doesn't necessarily dictate this happening, it does happen—because you care. Showing empathy to other teams who have a tough job or have to make tough decisions is a critical part of inclusion as well. They appreciate your rallying for reducing complexity and get behind changes you suggest making.

Being clear with expectations and communication is considered being resourceful by reducing the effect of chaos or misguided information that is causing things to slow down. This includes email communications and knowing when to just pick up the phone (my rule was, if three emails were exchanged and it was still churning, pick up the phone).

Always be learning. This is important in understanding not only what your company may offer to upskill yourself and team, but what they will support that is offered outside of the company. It never hurts to ask. This is one of the most resourceful methods I've used, not only in my corporate career, but in my new venture. Typically, once you start the process of seeking knowledge, so much will present itself to you. That includes people you may meet who can mentor or teach you, tools that you didn't know existed, and courses that can help you build and expand your knowledge base.

There are many other ways to put your resourcefulness to work for you, increasing your personal power and giving you the confidence to keep it.

Finding It and Keeping It

Personal power is somewhat of an unspoken component of our consciousness in the workplace, personal relationships, and community. In fact, it's probably one of the most important components that offers us personal happiness, balance, and the confidence to bring forward innovation. Ever feel like you were punched in the gut when someone shames you or tears down an idea you shared (and you thought was great)? That feeling was your personal power being drained by, yes, the person who challenged you. Why? Because we have been conditioned to fear the result or reaction and end up questioning ourselves, creating doubt. We took the feedback personally and gave away our power.

The word "power" is typically associated with certain titles, influence, or scope of authority. In reality, it's a lot more than that and does impact our opportunity to find, activate, and keep our own personal power. One of my goals is to use power in refined and elevated ways. How can we find love in power? I'll address "power programming," and then we'll jump into the components of personal power and how to activate your personal power.

Addressing our power programming. I think we should address a couple of things on the topic of power. Your "beliefs" around power should be cleared before you can find your personal power in a way that is aligned to your authenticity. Thinking back to childhood, what did power look like to you? What have you been conditioned to believe about power—power over people, power is evil, power is above all? Yes, power can be all of those things if not used in the best light, but it can also be beautiful, loving, and quiet. Power comes from truth. It can nourish people, projects, and plans, allowing us to give what is needed, when it is needed, and in appropriate amounts. Power should not be presumed to be only hierarchical or based on status, title, or financial position. It is more than that and important to address before journeying to finding and keeping your personal power.

Let's look at what healthy personal power is and how it can be used. Important considerations you may not link to the impact of your personal power include being supportive, collaborating, using tact, influencing situations or others, compromising, cooperating, setting healthy boundaries, being vulnerable, connecting with our inner authority, and using gentle power and persuasion.

Our personal power becomes a challenge when we control, use forceful displays, and showcase entitlement, directness, confrontation, victim mindset, manipulation, and money power over others. Finding and using our personal power in the most aligned way will provide us with the ability to keep it.

Emotional intelligence is an important key to personal power, and although we shifted from our minds ending the "age of reason" (in the late 1700s) into our emotional intelligence, we are still evolving. Examining our true self is a lifelong process.

Components of personal power. Personal power is an energy and energy source at its foundation. In some practices and beliefs dating back thousands of years in India, it is located in our third chakra (solar plexus or manipura chakra). It provides a source of personal power and relates to self-esteem, warrior energy, and the power of transformation. There are more modern concepts like Human Design which recognizes our G Center or Self/Identity Center. In this concept, we will attract into our life the experiences that will teach us how to expand—to love ourselves more deeply, stand in and embrace our personal power, express ourselves authentically, and let go of the past while simultaneously learning from it. When we are out of alignment, the Self/Identity Center attracts in lessons and tests that will push us back into alignment.

Let's get back to the question at the beginning of this chapter posed by Tony Robbins, "Who did you have to be to feel accepted or loved as a child?" How does that show up for you as an adult? Do you have patterns of self-sabotage, comparison, or dimming who you are to fit in? There are two challenges that may have continued this programming.

One of the challenges we are up against, whether intentional (society/advertising/media) or unintentional (family/teachers/friends), is the conditioning that has kept us small and thinking lack, not good enough, or too much! Another is fear. Finding courage to face our fears is foundational to finding our personal power. Are you afraid of rejection, looking bad, humiliation, being shamed, being embarrassed, making a mistake, or other fear that you feel holds you back?

It's so important we continue to check in on this programming and address it to allow us to not only gain our personal power, but keep it too!

Your personal power. Personal power is an ability to access and own your true potential where you recognize yourself as an individual who is the best version of who you are. It is realizing your authentic self with all your strengths and weaknesses, accepting yourself for who you are, and then defining for yourself how to use this power to achieve your goals.

Here are some key components to finding and keeping your personal power:

- *Develop a growth mindset.* It means looking for the positive, being open to new ways of thinking/doing/being, learning from each lesson, and paying attention to those lessons.
- *Identify* your needs, values, and beliefs so your actions align with your core. Align yourself with your values and act consistently with what you believe and who you believe you are.
- *Speak your truth* and just tell the truth; make it a habit. Vulnerability is such a trust-builder. Don't bullshit your way through conversations. You are not expected to know everything.

Keep things moving forward, continually growing both mentally and emotionally. This will help you to keep uncovering and strengthening your personal power. The satisfaction you achieve at work, the connections you make, and personal relationships you improve are worth the effort. Feeling more balanced and authentic will not only give you peace of mind, but allow the full you to show up every day.

Make the Shift

Here are some key areas to activate and keep your personal power:
- Define and state your goals, desires, and intentions.
- Be aware when you are being negative about yourself.
- Set healthy boundaries and maintain them.
- Speak up and share your ideas and thoughts.
- Maintain a growth mindset.
- Self-reflect daily.
- Advocate for yourself and others.
- Acknowledge and accept your fears—don't brush them under the rug.
- Ask for help and support—be vulnerable.

32

TAPPING INTO YOUR POWERS

Intuition is a very powerful thing, more powerful than intellect.
——Steve Jobs

The Tools of Self

Self-discovery is something you can continue to evolve through investigating those earlier questions about what holds you back from being your authentic self and determining why you feel you can't be your authentic self. I view this as a never-ending process. Continue to hone your core values and beliefs. Get to know yourself in a way that is deeper than you thought. Who are you really? Who do you want to be? What are the differences, and what can you do to close the gap?

Self-knowledge is more about knowing yourself. What do you need, and what makes you tick? It's becoming friends with yourself and being so close to yourself that you know exactly what you need in any particular situation, no matter what the experts are saying. It's important to connect in order to know yourself. This is where your intuition can come through, your inner knowing. It's that sense that brings you in and out of situations and where you can tap into making decisions. You can use discernment to check in with whether "something is yours." Does it belong to you, or have you picked it up from something or someone else?

Self-acceptance is one of the biggest issues most of us have, mainly because we are taught growing up and in the corporate environment to fit into the box in how we show up, behave, perform, and just be. We are taught to be small, think small, don't show up too much, or we need to tone it down. We are fearful of making a mistake, being shamed, and not accepted because of who we genuinely are. I'm quirky, geeky, share much of my personal likes (that are not mainstream), and get excited about the little things in life. I've accepted these things about myself, although I was fearful of not being accepted when I was a young adult. I honestly don't care anymore. I find accepting myself and not hiding who I am has given permission to others to do the same. I also try to embrace these qualities in each person in my world. It's what makes us unique! Where do you struggle with self-acceptance, and how can you overcome it? Let go of expectations and ideologies. How can you accept yourself for the imperfect human you are?

Self-awareness sounds like a well-used term. Typically, though, it is utilized in conversations that are actually negatively based. Be more self-aware of how you speak your message and how you behave. Negative, negative, freaking negative! Instead, let's use this as a superpower to ensure we are being our authentic self. Is what we are saying and doing matching up to what we believe and with who we are? If not, then it can be used positively to get us back on track. Identify your passions, strengths, talents, and gifts and build on them. Understand more about how others see you. It's important to be present and have value-added connections with family, friends, and co-workers.

Self-reflection and evaluation is crucial to deciphering the complexities of your authentic self. You can equip yourself to focus on building yourself up on qualities that distinguish you and your personal power. Train your brain to ask why, what, when, where, which, who, and will? Are the words you speak and actions you take actually necessary? Getting back to creating a daily practice of self-reflection is one of the best ways I've found to grow.

Self-adaptation is also important and necessary as you evolve, based on your environment and your personal stories. Your personal power is strong and based on who you are currently, so ensure adaptation is in alignment with your authenticity and emotional intelligence. This will also be important in the workplace as you evolve your elevated gifts.

Self-activation of your personal power depends on the work you have done (above topics). What emotions do you feel when your personal power is strong? Is it being threatened? This is something I physically feel. Typically, I feel upset in my stomach area (solar plexus chakra) or tightening in my throat (throat chakra). Listen to your body and tune into its messages. This is part of your intuition gift and will be very valuable as you activate your elevated gifts.

Tap Into Your Intuition and the "Clairs"

Intuition is a process that gives us information without conscious analysis. It can appear in the form of sudden flashes of thought, feeling, or inspiration. It's an ability that bridges knowledge between our conscious and our subconscious mind. How can you tell the difference between your intuition telling you something important, and your mind getting carried away and obsessing over something unimportant?

Intuition for most people is "less verbal" and more silent and textural. It's more like a feeling, knowing, or vibration. Your intuition is loving. It's a gentle and kind nudge toward positivity and warmth. With intuition, you just "know" something. It doesn't need to make sense. It doesn't need a logical explanation. It's a flash of inspiration, a sudden impulse, a "gut feeling." When we play, we allow the right and left hemispheres of our brain to activate. When we do things without being attached to the outcome, ideas, clarity, guidance, and solutions have the space to drop in. This is when we make space for our intuition. Meditation is another method to do so. The answers we seek are within us already. Tap into that massive superpower!

When the ego mind is at work, mental chatter and overanalysis is "chattier." It's noisier and often repetitive (the same thoughts cycle over and over for hours, days, or weeks). When we find balance and are able to quiet our mind, our intuition can present itself.

There are other gifts that support the elevated gifts, and understanding these gifts helps to leverage your intuition. Most call them the "Clairs" (senses) that are commonly used for intuiting messages via your sixth sense.[21] Typically, people resonate with one or up to a few of these Clair gifts. Here is a quick rundown of the more popular ones. Which of these do you immediately resonate with? Let your intuition help you out.

Clairvoyance, or clear vision, allows you to reach into another vibrational frequency and visually perceive "within the mind's eye." This may include images or symbols in your head, almost like a movie playing in your mind. You tend to use the phrase, "I see." You have a good imagination. You are an expert at problem-solving and puzzles. You see patterns. You have active or vivid dreams.

Clairaudience, or clear audio/hearing, allows you to perceive sounds or words and extrasensory noise in your head, almost like it's your own voice. You tend to use the phrases, "I hear you," or "I hear what you're saying." You prefer to listen, read, or research things. Music helps you connect. You often converse with yourself or mumble something out loud.

Clairsentience, or clear sensation or feeling, allows you to perceive information by a "feeling" within the whole body, without any outer stimulus related to the feeling or information. You tend to use the phrase, "I feel" or "I sense that ...." You prefer to experience things. Large crowds and loud noise drains you. You are sensitive to energies around you.

---

[21] Team Blog, "Are You A Clairvoyant, Clairaudient, Claircognizant, Or Clairsentience?" *Exhale Meditation Studio,* https://enhalems.com/communication/

Claircognizance, or clear knowing, allows you to just have a knowing about things. For many strong in this gift, it feels like knowledge pours into the top of their heads. You tend to use phrases such as, "I know ... ," "I don't know how, but I just know somehow." Intuition and gut feeling are elevated. You pick up on some skills very easily. Your mind is full of ideas and possibilities. Answers and solutions come easily to you.

Clairempathy, or clear emotion, allows you to physically tune into the emotional experience, attitudes, or physical ailments of a person, place, or animal. People say you're too sensitive. You pick up on moods of others. This doesn't involve rational thinking, logic, deduction, or reason. It's a spontaneous energetic perception. You feel physical sensations in your body and emotions in your mind.

You can tap into your "Clairs" when you seek to tap into your intuition, the best words to say, to understand, make a connection, clarity or guidance, to solve a problem, or find a solution.

Make the Shift

Let's determine which of the Clairs you resonate with most.

1. Which Clair(s) felt immediate to you?
2. Have you previously known this was your gift? If not, are you surprised?
3. Think back to when you last used this gift, but didn't realize this was how you knew.
4. In what ways in your daily life can you focus on using your Clair(s)?

33

YOUR GIFTS TAKE SHAPE

If you're always trying to be normal you will never know how amazing you can be.

——Maya Angelou

Identifying Your Elevated Gifts

You have done a lot of exploring, deep dives, and inner work throughout this book, identifying areas that resonate with you, may cause limitation, and hold you back from being your authentic self in the workplace. You are ready to identify your elevated gifts. You have them within you. They are waiting to shine. If you have not taken the quiz included with the free bonuses with this book, go to www.angiemccourt.com/loveyourgifts and take the quiz now. It's a fun way to get things started. While you're there download the workbook, if you have not done so, to help with this section.

What was the result of your number one elevated gift? Were you surprised? Did it feel at home to know this, or was it uncomfortable? How did it feel in your body? Did it feel like excitement, nervousness, or calmness? Welcome in your elevated gift and embrace it. There is still work to do, so don't worry. Now that you know what it feels like when you resonate with your number one elevated gift, which of the other gifts give you the most sensation and reaction? Continue going through each one and determine how many more you resonate with. Below is a bit of a guide to help you. Clear your space, time, and mind to really go through the guide.

Make the Shift

Here is a guide to your elevated gifts.

Évocateur—Have you been called a dreamer? Do you have flashes of ideas that play around like the cosmos in your mind? Do you get excited when you bring a new idea forward? Do you struggle with actually making your big ideas happen? Do you find partnering with someone who can strategize and help execute your ideas exciting? Do you get others excited about your ideas?

Edgewalker—Do you get deeply passionate about causes? Do you listen to the collective group or team for what they are struggling with? Do you believe in a future state that is better than today (program, process, culture, model), and are you not afraid to share your ideas about it? Do you struggle with getting others to make the leap to the future state? Do you feel like you have one foot in the here and now and one foot in the future, Or always walking on the edge?

Storyteller—do you take your time to create a story around an idea you want to share? Do you tie in all aspects in a cohesive way? Do you use words and messaging that relate to your audience? Is your idea clear and accepted? How do you feel in your body when you successfully deliver an idea that is received fully (even if it's not agreed to)?

Networker—do you see the connections you make with and between others as a form of synchronicity? Are you open to the message a new connection may have for you, or you for them? Do you let it flow? Do you foresee the impact any connection can have and how you can influence that path? Can you strategically see how bridging two groups or more can help solve problems? Are your engagements selfless?

Servant Leader—what is the most important characteristic you cherish about your favorite leader? Does it involve autonomy, accountability, ownership, vulnerability, humility, or compassion for others? Do you seek truth and include others in solving problems? Do you trust others and are you trusted by others?

Seeker—where would you gage your integrity? Are you honest? Do your actions match your words and match your core values? Are you transparent and clear on your expectations? Do you follow through on your word and commitments? Do you stay true to yourself even when there is pressure (especially in a hierarchical structure)? Do you engage with others without a personal agenda? Do you deliver on your goals in an ethical way?

Messenger—do others come to you to knowing you will represent their ideas or concerns? Do you feel comfortable, or not, bringing them forward? Do you feel the message within your body that you need to deliver? Do the messages you need to deliver just "come" to you?

Transmitter—do ideas, solutions, and information flow through you when you are speaking, writing, or creating presentations? Have you ever wondered where "that" came from as you had literally never thought of it before? Do you sometimes zone out (in a good way) when presenting or addressing a group? Have solutions popped into your head, clear as day, when helping a colleague solve a problem, or when providing clarity or guidance?

Creator—do you feel you are strategic? Do you create a plan from an idea and articulate it clearly so it can successfully be executed? Are you grounded in understanding people's (customers/colleagues/partners) abilities, desires, and needs? Are you aware of looking for impacts upstream and downstream in an organization, process, or business model to ensure there are no "gotchas"? Do you bring new plans to the table including business, team, organizational, and cultural? Do you see all components that need to be included to be successful? Are you considerate of change management and training?

Generator—are you kick-ass at getting sh$t done (GSD)? Do you see how something needs to happen and quickly add your process to get it done? Do you get excited to get your hands dirty? Do you enjoy watching progress being made? Do you relish getting results? Do you connect with the Creator's vision and strategy easily? Do you feel your value when you see the results of your work?

Experimenter—do you look at a challenge as an opportunity? Do you look past failure or something looking bad to what could be? Do you see how an experiment should go? Are you able to get buy-in from others through experimenting? Are you inclusive in your experiments?

Collaborator—do you consider all parties that may be impacted? Do you push others to be inclusive? Do you know when to be inclusive? Do you see the power of inclusivity? Are you the first one to call out when a group or person can provide valuable insight or feedback, even though it's not popular?

Influencer—are you aligned with your core values and priorities when making decisions? Do you feel confident in knowing what you want? Are you self-assured in your abilities? Are you clear in speaking about what you want and in making choices? Do you stick to your decisions? Do you hold yourself accountable to your decisions and choices?

Logician—do you take calculated risks? Do you challenge old ways of evaluating risk? Do you have a process for collecting information and input in making decisions around risks? Do you bring a bigger picture to the conversation versus just financial information? Do you trust your gut? Do you tap into your intuition as part of your information-gathering? Do you challenge data with wisdom and knowing? Do you hold yourself accountable for ensuring success?

Liberator—are you the first one to speak up about something that needs change? Do you follow your truth? Do you empower others to seek theirs? Do you show the benefits of making changes? Do you support others who are not being treated fairly? Do you see through bull$hit?

Challenger—do you challenge the status quo? Do you bring others down a path of realization that there is a better way? Do you challenge old systems/models? Do you bring new ideas and solutions to the conversation? Do you listen to the health of the business and team and determine what needs to be changed? Do you show no fear when bringing issues forward because you passionately believe in making a difference?

Wow that was intense! I suggest going back through that section again and revisit your workbook responses as well. This is a journey, and once an elevated gift is utilized more fully, you will find other gifts shining through that may not have resonated yet.

Using Your Gifts in the Workplace

I'm going to start this guidance with a bit of a disclaimer. Every environment is different. Every manager is different. Every company culture is different. Most of these differences are either set by current leadership or, more than likely, carried over from years of old models and culture. You should use judgment when determining how to share your elevated gifts in your environment. Remember, this is not about forcing something. This is about authentic self.

When your intentions are true (whether others agree with your message or not), you are in authenticity. You may not have the most popular message to share or it may not be "right," but delivering it in a respectful way definitely helps to keep you in balance. When your intentions are pure (not selfish), others trust you. Others will look to you to be the light that gives them hope—the one whom they will follow regardless of your title or role—because you shine brightly in your authentic skin.

Remember, a big part of your elevated gift unveiling is that you are breaking out of the box. You are bringing your full self to the table, and you are respectfully declining the invitation to be like everyone else.

Determine your own path and not one dictated by managers, leaders, or assumed expectations. Learn about what interests you. Get involved with other teams to better understand their challenges and how you can help. Don't go from the box into a bubble.

Being aware of your "audience" and how they receive information or deal with change is an input to how you deliver that message. Sometimes things need to be broken down into bite-size pieces so others can get on board with you. Sometimes it can take a long time (even years) until the audience is ready to hear. Sometimes it takes a new audience to understand the vision. Be patient and don't get too disappointed. You role may only be delivering the message or idea, and someone else's job to carry it forward. Stay connected to the bigger picture, and share your ideas, concerns, and solutions with many.

The workplace is only one area of life in which to use your gifts! Some elevated gifts may be more relevant outside of the workplace. Nevertheless, your authentic self belongs in every part of your life.

34

YOUR METHODOLOGY

Pay attention to the gift and the world will pay attention to you.
——Nicky Verd

Activating Your Elevated Gifts

If you feel comfortable, share one new thing that is *authentically you* with your team. Is it an interest or desire? Is it an experience from your past? Do what you feel comfortable doing, but bringing down the shield and opening up can help you ease into your authentic self. There is no timeline, so take your time. Be methodical, if you'd like. Pick the people that you feel connected to when sharing.

Slow down and be present. Find quiet space and time, even if it's short. This is really tough if you are a fast-paced, task-oriented, or overcommitted person. It's OK, you can do it! You will love it. There is no guilt here, you're not missing out on anything, nor are you dropping the ball. You are here, now. Do this exercise to get fully present mindfully. It's called the 5-4-3-2-1. Acknowledge five things you can see around you. Then acknowledge four things you can touch around you. Acknowledge three things you can hear around you. Acknowledge two things you can smell around you and one thing you can taste around you.

Laugh [22] and don't take yourself too seriously! When was the last time you laughed, like really belly-laughed? Laughter stimulates your heart and other major organs. Just a moment of laughter allows us to think more clearly and creatively and raises relatedness with our colleagues. According to an article on TheConversation.com:

> "Laughter—doing it or observing it—activates multiple regions of the brain: the motor cortex, which controls muscles; the frontal lobe, which helps you understand context; and the limbic system, which modulates positive emotions. Turning all these circuits on strengthens neural connections and helps a healthy brain coordinate its activity."[23]

Bring more laughter to your workplace and team. Just laugh out loud.

Meditation is a great way to tap into your inner, higher self and seek clarity, or guidance, or just clear the space for it to come at another time. Ask yourself, "I seek clarity of my elevated gifts, what am I supposed to share with the world?"

Use your *self-awareness* tool and practice this daily. How did you respond to something or someone? Did you react or did you feel a spark when an idea hit you hard? Did you let it go, yet are curious about it? What made you feel whole or incomplete? What can you do to explore it? What feels unfinished to you?

Stop holding your breath. Our breath is our life force. It's how we activate our body, heart, organs, and brain. It's also how we release toxins from our body, so it's as important to fully breathe out as it is in. Practice breathing deeply and see what happens. Use your belly (not chest) to breathe and connect to your breath. Picture yourself breathing in

[22] Gabriel Berezin, Mika Liss, "The Neuroscience of Laughter, and How to Inspire More of It at Work"- Your Brain At Work (blog), *Neuro Leadership Institute, September 17, 2020,* https://neuroleadership.com/your-brain-at-work/neuroscience-laughter-at-work/

[23] Janet M. Gibson, Team Blog, "Laughing is good for your mind and your body – here's what the research shows," The Conversation, https://theconversation.com/laughing-is-good-for-your-mind-and-your-body-heres-what-the-research-shows-145984

inspiration and breathing out what you no longer need in your life or body.

Pay attention to your body, as it is the temple that will give you intuitive feedback. Where in your body do you feel responses to things you see, feel, touch, or hear? Connect with that part and feeling so you can more easily recognize it in the future. If your elevated gifts are trying to emerge but fear is holding you back, being able to recognize that in your body will help you realize it's time to move past it and work on the root issue.

Take action. What's one thing you would love to bring forward at work—something you feel in your bones or that just won't leave you alone? Test out how you would bring this forward, and take your time. Observe the reactions/responses of others. Find a quiet place after sharing, and review what you observed. Let it sink in. What could you tweak? How did it feel?

Observe others. Now that you know what some of these elevated gifts look like, observe those around you to see if they are practicing any of these gifts. Appreciate them for shining, and even ask if they can guide you. They may not even realize they are showcasing a special gift.

Repeat any and all of the above regularly. The key is to stay connected to yourself and aligned, and embody your true authentic self. This unlocks your elevated gifts.

Adapting Your Elevated Gifts

Let's start with a definition of adapting according to the *Oxford English Dictionary:* "Make (something) suitable for a new use or purpose; modify." Nowhere in this definition is "dim your light." Adapting does not mean conform back to the old ways. It means align it with your current environment, culture, and support system. There are so many levels of intensity our elevated gifts can be used with, and in some environments, the more intense, the better. In others, subtlety wins every time. So how do you know which intensity level you need to bring with your gift to be most effective?

This is where you bring in your other tools, your intuition, awareness, and observation of your own body. Does it feel like too much or not enough? Do you hear a whisper saying, "bring it"? Do you see others responding at a less intense level? Are you resonating with others? Your elevated gifts can be adapted based on how your audience is responding and based on how intense you may need to be, depending on who needs to hear the message or idea.

There is potentially a period of time you may need to adapt to your authenticity and elevated gifts as well. Give yourself space and time. Continue to use your activation practices to feed your adaptation. Remember, adapting does not mean to dim your light, be small, or change who you are. It means to be aware of your surroundings and what is necessary to show up with, and adjust as needed.

Work Your Challenges

I call the somewhat negative or overdoing it parts of elevated gifts "challenges." Challenges are not bad, they are just something to be aware of and work on to stay in balance. Typically, the challenges come through when some piece of the gift falls away from your authentic self. It's when fear invades your elevated gift in some way, or when ego gets a little too much power. Being aware of and acknowledging when this is happening gives you back your power to find balance and get back to true intentions and authenticity.

We are human, perfect in all of our imperfections, and so the challenges will enter the elevated gifts in all of us. Our elevated gifts are not effective when we lose sight of our authentic intentions, ignore the challenges, or live in them instead. They can be disruptive and ineffective. When you were working on ways to adapt your gifts, you may have had some fear come across your mind. Will this fear cause you to dim your light or shut down your elevated gift? This is part of working your challenges as well. If you refer back to each gift, I offered some suggestions of observations I've had over the years or experienced myself of how these challenges might come across. Use this as a guide and explore your own gifts deeper from there.

Make the Shift

How to work your challenges:

1. Find equanimity to start. Equanimity as defined by the *Oxford English Dictionary* as: (noun) mental calmness, composure, and evenness of temper, especially in a difficult situation.

2. Take a step back. Pause. Quiet your mind.

3. Check in with your intentions. Are they still aligned to passion, core values, and the "why" this gift is needed?

4. Let go of ego attachment to outcomes. These are probably showing up as control, perfection, and being right. Tell yourself you don't need to be right, and show compassion for what your elevated gift is working to do.

5. Ask yourself from a place of intuitive embodiment, is this the right place and time to share my elevated gift? Is this the most effective way I want to show up with my elevated gift at this time?

Supporting Others' Elevated Gifts in Action

Once you become aware of these elevated gifts, you will start to recognize them in your daily life. One of the opportunities to revolutionize authenticity in the workplace is by supporting each other on our own journeys, acknowledging and appreciating these gifts as we see their impact in the workplace, guiding and supporting through the challenges work, and encouraging others to appreciate someone you see sharing their gifts. Too often I've seen and practiced many of these gifts, yet they are not appreciated for the results they bring. They become expected and "just part of that person's abilities." Enough is enough. These elevated gifts are blooming. They are breaking through their traditional constraints. They are shifting and allowing us to truly be in our authentic skin.

Now is the time to slow down, be aware, and call out what you see coming through in others. They will do the same for you. It doesn't matter if the highest ranked person in the room gets it. The person who is supposed to receive your support and message will get it. Loud and clear. You will empower and enable others through your support, understanding, encouragement, and confidence in their elevated gifts blooming too.

We are all here to support each other. Comparison and competition is dead by now, and your viewpoints of authenticity encourage supporting each other instead. Trust your intuition to guide you. Listen and ask questions. Talk about your elevated gifts. Share your struggles and how you have overcome them. Be the living example of how these gifts can shine and you "can" show up authentically.

I've been very vocal about many of my elevated gifts with students of the Exploratory Lab Boot Camp program to try to keep them OUT of the box and holding on to their authentic self as they enter the professional environment. I also have led by example for my teams over the years to encourage them to shine in their elevated gifts as well. This is one of the most effective ways I've found to support others. It's the silent challenge to dig deep into themselves and let go of their limitations.

Make the Shift

Pick someone to support. Then another and another. Lead by example.

- Identify someone you have regular visibility of or access to whom you see with blooming elevated gifts.
- Show public support (start in small settings and then bigger ones) for their courage and creative inputs. Back them up.

- Give guidance behind the scenes if you see they need just a little nudge or may be struggling with a challenge.
- Ask for support for yourself if you feel you need someone's guidance.
- Lead by example and let your elevated gifts shine. Talk about them. Talk about your process for embracing your gift(s).

Be Purposeful

Your elevated gifts are blooming because the world needs them and you. The workplace needs a revamp, and authenticity is not a buzz word. It's what keeps us purposeful. It's what allows us to connect to what and where we work. It's what gives us our value, individuality, and connection to the collective. It's how we contribute in a unique way. Being purposeful is how we ensure our intentions stay true and get to impactful results. That may be as simple as helping someone make a connection to a job, or creating an entirely new business model that is more aligned with what customers need.

Being purposeful is one of the ways we deliver our elevated gifts to the workplace or other area of our life. It's also how we stay in our personal power in an authentic way. Finding purpose is something many seek. How about instead thinking about how you can live a purposeful life in everything you do? How is that possible and how does your path unfold? It all ties back to your authentic, true self. Staying aligned to who you are helps you live purposefully, which aligns you to your path.

Watch your path unfold as you continue on your journey. I've found there is not one path either. It twists and winds and changes based on your growth and readiness within your initiation of life. Stay open, believe in yourself and others, and keep things simple. Read the signs, embrace the synchronicities, go through the open doors, be curious, and know that you are on a journey that is purposeful. You are purposeful.

35

THE REVOLUTION

Always ask yourself if what you're doing today is getting you closer to
where you want to be tomorrow.
——Paul Coelho

The New Checkbox

There is an opportunity to change how the checkboxes of abilities, skills, and talents are recognized in the systems that exist inside of corporations. These have existed for a long time. They have been replicated across organizations over the past hundred years as the industrial revolution set the stage. The old ways of hierarchical and patriarchal structure and constructs may have worked for that time. Yet they have not evolved to catch up to the current times.

The traditional annual performance reviews with the same expectations of everyone regardless of your job, experience, or abilities shoves everyone in the same box, creating competition and comparison. It's time to change this practice to a more fluid and natural engagement between manager and employee. Training managers to build their coaching skills if they are managing people is a great start. Getting rid of the scripted guidelines on how to have a conversation, show up authentically, and fluidly engage, connect with, encourage, and appreciate the authentic person sitting across the table is the goal.

Performance reviews and performance management systems are in need of changing. According to Gallup, "To stay valuable to employers, workers will need to spend more time doing things machines have a hard time with—things like taking initiative, creatively solving problems, collaborating effectively and across teams in their organizations to maximize their contributions. In turn, organizations will need to adjust their management systems to allow for greater employee autonomy and flexibility, while maintaining accountability and high productivity."[24] I love their resulting recommendations that the most important thing to performance management in the coming years is (1) that the correct outcomes are identified, and (2) gaining acceptance by employees and being transparent on performance measurement.

Changing the "checkbox" of performance and developmental items will open up possibilities to allow for elevated gifts to shine and a more effective shift to happen in the workplace and in business. If you no longer fit the "checkbox," start the conversation with human resources, your manager, and team. What would be ideal to use as a gauge?

Every environment is different, and current skills of management vary significantly. My suggestion is that this becomes a two-way review. When sharing any expectation, the question should be asked, "How can I help, or what do you need?" Does the environment allow you to be your authentic self? Is there a skill you would like to enhance? Are you aligned with your goals? Do you need clarity on anything in order to achieve them?

What does the person need to be able to increase their skills, bring new ideas or solutions to the table, and empowerment to achieve results? Then, how are they owning it? Are they taking proactive action to contribute to the evolving expectations of the business? Are they bringing forward

---

[24] Jake Herway, "The Performance Management Needs of the Changing Workforce" *Gallup, June 26, 2018,* https://www.gallup.com/workplace/240578/performance-management-needs-changing-workforce.aspx

solutions along with challenges or issues? Are they teaming up and influencing others to find a bigger solution? Are they courageous in how they bring important messages forward on behalf of the whole? Are they showing acts of intentional inclusiveness that effectively expands the outcome? Do they leverage effective communication to bring clarity and alignment to a situation or opportunity? Do they anticipate what is needed and fully commit to resolving it, or do they piecemeal or hand off to others to finish? Do they speak in metaphors to get their point across effectively? Are they open about when they just "know" or "feel" something is right? Do they speak up when something should be addressed?

Creating a different approach to the traditional "checkbox" performance management systems to put ownership on both employee and management provides an opportunity to increase trust, productivity, and engagement. When employees feel connected to not only their role or company, but to their manager in a trusting way, they will stay. They will commit.

Conclusion

In conclusion, as our own human evolution is activated, we have now shifted from the intellectual age into an age of energy. This allows us to be more connected to our body, heart, and self, and not so much to external forces or validation. We are learning to trust ourselves and unlock our elevated gifts and authentic self. We are being called to do so.

Life is not a "one problem-one solution" equation. It's a complex spider web finely crafted to both protect us and ensure we grow. Every turn can create a new opportunity for growth and discovery. Every path leads us closer to our next stage. We are evolving and ever-changing. We are human. We are connected. We are unique and we are love.

Living at this time is so special and a great opportunity to be part of making the shifts needed to move into the next stage of evolution. Our minds can expand, and our hearts can too. It's about showing up in our authentic skin and embracing our elevated gifts. That's how we make the changes needed in order to improve life and happiness as we know it, and to bring a better balance to the crazy, beautiful world and work.

These concepts will allow every person to bloom and embrace their authenticity. Not some in-the-box, phony, made up, social media-influenced self, but the self within. The higher self.

Thank you for taking the time to read this book and embrace the work to unlock your elevated gifts. I'm so proud of you and look forward to watching you bloom. This world needs you.

ACKNOWLEDGMENTS

I'm so grateful for my parents and their support over the years of my career, raising my own family and encouraging me to be true to myself. Thank you Kristi, Andrea, Amanda, Diana, Bill, Mom, Brandon, Hunter, Blake, Gia and others who have specifically contributed to feedback and topic inclusion during this book writing journey.

Thank you to my amazing crew of experts whom I could not have birthed this book without. Thank you Heidi Eliason of Runaway Publishing for guidance and a big education during the editing and proofreading phases. You made this book and its message even more impactful. Thank you Lauren Diamond for all of the graphics work you created to help me with the many projects I have launched including this book cover. Thank you Shawna Benson for a fun photo shoot in Montana where we were able to capture the book back cover and website photos.

I'd like to thank all of the mentors, teachers, guidss and those who inspired me with their missions and work over the years. There are too many to name. I'd also like to acknowledge the many mentees who guided me as much as I guided them over the years.

Thank you to so many friends who have supported me over the recent events of my son's passing. This was really hard to keep this book going, but I realized how much it can help others and my job was to get it out into the world. My son Brandon was so excited about this book and I know he is proud.

Thank you to my love, partner and best friend John. You have been amazing on this journey. Thank you for your support, love and space to bring this to life. I love life with you.

Bibliography

Below is a list of books that has shaped my learning.

Haddock, Jack H., (2015). *The Subconscious Mind: How to Unlock the Powerful Force of Your Subconscious Mind.* Createspace Independent Publishing Platform.

Swart, Tara (MD, PhD), (2019). *The Source: The Secrets of the Universe, the Science of the Brain.* Harper One.

Campbell, Rebecca, (2016). *Rise Sister Rise: A Guide to Unleashing The Wise, Wild Woman Within.* Hay House UK.

Hendricks, Gay, (2009). *The Big Leap: Conquer Your Hidden Fear and Take Life to the Next Level.* Harper One.

Singer, Michael A., (2007). *The Untethered Soul: The Journey Beyond Yourself.* New Harbinger Publications.

Shetty, Jay, (2020). *Think Like a Monk: Train Your Mind for PEACE and PURPOSE Every day.* Simon & Schuster.

Gilbert, Elizabeth, (2015). *Big Magic: Creative Living Beyond Fear.* Riverhead Books.

Dweck, Carol S., (2006). *Mindset: The New Psychology of Success.* Random House.

McKeown, Greg, (2011). *Essentialism: The Disciplined Pursuit of Less.* Crown Business.

Bernstein, Gabrielle, (2018). *Judgment Detox: Release the Beliefs That Hold You Back from Living a better Life.* Gallery Books.

Chopra, Deepak, (2002). *Reinventing the Body, Resurrecting the Soul: How to Create a New You*. Harmony.

Bernstein, Gabrielle, (2019). *Super Attractor: Methods for Manifesting a Life Beyond Your Wildest Dreams*. Hay House.

Ambrosini, Melissa, (2016). *Mastering Your Mean Girl: The no BS guide to Silencing Your Inner Critic and becoming wildly Wealthy, fabulously Healthy and bursting with Love*. TarcherPerigee

Godin, Seth, (2008). *Tribes: We Need You to Lead Us*. Portfolio.

Robbins, Mel, (2017). *The 5 Second Rule: Transform Your Life, Work, and Confidence with Everyday Courage*. Savio Republic

Sincero, Jen, (2018). *You are a Badass Every Day: How to Keep Your Motivation Strong, Your Vibe High, and Your Quest for Transformation Unstoppable*. Penguin Life.

Hsieh, Tony, (2010). *Delivering Happiness: A Path to Profits, Passion and Purpose*. Grand Central Publishing.

Brown, Brene, (2008). *I Thought it was Just Me (but it isn't): Telling the Truth About Perfectionism, Inadequacy and power*. Gotham Books.

Sinek, Simon, (2014). *Leaders Eat Last*. Portfolio.

Sinek, Simon (2009). *Start With Why: How Great leaders Inspire Everyone To Take Action*. Portfolio.

Brown, Brene, (2015). *Rising Strong: How the Ability to Reset Transforms the Way We Live, Love, Parent, and Lead*. Spiegel & Grau.

Pressfield, Steven, (2002). *The War of Art: Winning The Inner Creative Battle*. Warner Books.

Granger, Jennifer, (2014). *Feminine Lost: Why Most Women are Male*. Hachette Books.

Kelley, Tom; Kelley, David, (2013). *Creative Confidence: Unleashing the Creative Potential Within Us All*. Crown Business.

There are so many other resources including Newsletters, online courses and live courses I have learned so much from over the years.

Going Deeper

If you're new to Authentic Me Revolution Coaching, let me introduce myself! I'm Angie McCourt your new Success + Mindset Coach.

I've shifted from 27 years in the corporate world into the helping industry at a time when people are looking to live purposeful.

The reason I wrote this book was to bring to light the struggles so many of us have in the workplace and all of those struggles that keep us from showing up as our authentic self. It's time to make the shift!

I want you to *BRIDGE THE GAP BETWEEN WHO + WHERE YOU ARE TO WHO + WHERE YOU WANT TO BE.*
I want you to *SHIFT YOUR MINDSET FROM LACK + LIMITATIONS TO SUCCESS + HAPPINESS*
I want you to *CREATE A VISION, STRATEGY AND PLAN TO ACHIEVE YOUR GOALS*
I want you to *BUILD AUTHENTIC, TRUSTING RELATIONSHPIS BY BEING YOUR TRUE AUTHENTIC SELF.*
I want you to *KICK THAT IMPOSTER SYNDROME AND SELF DOUBT IN THE BOOTY AND FEEL CONFIDENT.*
I want you to *ESTABLISH NEW HABITS THAT HELP YOU SUSTAIN A BALANCED SELF*

Check out my website www.angiemcourt.com/loveyourgifts where you can sign up for my Newsletter and schedule coaching sessions
Money Energy Reset Course www.angiemccourt.com/courses
Podcast – Shifting Inside Out on Spotify, Apple and Stitch

About the Author

Angie McCourt is an Author, Host of Shifting Inside Out podcast and Founder, Success + Mindset Coach of Authentic Me Revolution. She shifted from a 27-year career as a successful business leader into the helping industry at a time where major change can happen including revolutionizing the workplace and life in general. As a Success + Mindset Coach she helps clients shift their limiting beliefs and discover their elevated gifts so they can show up as their true self.

She is an Edgewalker, Seeker and Messenger discovered along her own journey of personal transformation. She has challenged status quo throughout her career and work in the community.

This is her first published book and has an online course called Money Energy Reset focusing on our relationship with money and the limitations that hold us back from achieving our dreams.

Angie's mission is to help others discover their gifts, be true to their self and find joy through mindset shift and actions to create the life they want to live.

Visit www.angiemccourt.com
Follow on Instagram @Angie_McCourt
Follow on LinkedIn @Angie McCourt